Charles Lord Hawkesbury

A Discourse on the Conduct of the Government of Great Britain

in Respect to Neutral Nations

Charles Lord Hawkesbury

A Discourse on the Conduct of the Government of Great Britain
in Respect to Neutral Nations

ISBN/EAN: 9783337304096

Printed in Europe, USA, Canada, Australia, Japan

Cover: Foto ©Suzi / pixelio.de

More available books at **www.hansebooks.com**

Printed for J. DE... BURLINGTON HOUSE, ...LY.

1794

ADVERTISEMENT.

THE following difcourfe was written in 1757 by Charles Jenkinson, Efq. now Lord Hawkesbury. Great Britain was at that time engaged in war with France, and the Republic of Holland refufed to conform to thofe treaties of defenfive alliance, by which fhe was then bound to affift Great Britain, and fuffered her fubjects not only to trade with France, but to afford protection to the property of the enemy; to fupply him with naval and military ftores, and to bring to the French ports in Europe the produce of the French Weft India iflands. The Britifh government ordered all Dutch fhips, laden with the property of the enemy, or with naval or military ftores, or with the produce of the French

French West India islands, to be seized, and to be brought into port for legal adjudication. The merchants of Holland remonstrated against this measure, which deprived them of a most lucrative trade; but the British government persevered. This DISCOURSE was written in support of the principles on which the BRITISH GOVERNMENT at that time acted. It was translated and re-printed in almost every language of Europe; and it is now re-published, from the best edition, at the desire of several noblemen and gentlemen, who think, that in the present circumstances it may be equally useful.

Piccadilly, Jan. 27, 1794.

A DISCOURSE, &c.

IT is unhappy for the race of mankind, that those collective bodies, into which it is divided, should be subject to the same passions and animosities, as the individuals, of which they are composed, and not have, like them, some visible superior tribunal, which might hear and compose their dissensions: this might, perhaps, prevent those appeals, which are too frequently made to the sword, where the events of war alone decide the cause, and the sentence, which passeth on the transgressor, brings also to the injured party a large share of misfortunes in the execution of it. The welfare of mankind however requires, that this necessary evil should be confined within the narrowest bounds; and that a trial, where the proceedings are so destructive, should be made as short and as equitable as the nature of it will admit: it is the duty therefore of those who are not concerned in the dispute to be extremely attentive to their conduct, that they may not thereby contribute to render the contest unequal: as far as man is concerned, it is force alone on which the decision depends; to add therefore, by any means, to the power of one party is manifest injustice to the other, and is besides highly injurious to the rest of mankind, since it necessarily tends to spread discord among nations, and from a single spark of contention to light up a general flame.

It might be hoped, that a duty like this, inforced by such powerful motives, would be universally observed; and that no private inferior interest could induce any power to transgress it; if some little profits, the object of greedy individuals, should, perhaps, arise from the violation of it; can a nation in general reap a benefit, where public justice receives a wound? To act in opposition to this, in hopes of some present advantage, is to establish a dangerous example, which may hereafter prove injurious to ourselves; it is to untie the only band, which holdeth nations happily together, and to banish mutual confidence

fidence from the various communities of the world.

Such, however, hath been the mistaken conduct of some neutral states during the present war.—France consented to the treaty of Aix-la-Chappele, that she might the more securely pursue the objects of her ambition; and that under the disguise of peace she might extend and fortify her possessions in a part of the world, where her arms in time of open war had always, till then, been unsuccessful: for this purpose she had artfully contrived, that the American rights should not be determined by that treaty, but be left to the consideration of commissaries, to whose decisions she never meant to pay any regard.— Canada was her vulnerable part : this therefore she resolved first to strengthen, and then to enter again with more confidence into war; while we were employed in debating our rights, she took more effectual means to end the contest in her favour; she sent frequent supplies to America; she seized and fortified the passes and navigable rivers of that country, drove the English from their possessions, and built forts on the dominions of Great Britain; when the design was thus far advanced, England saw it in all its terrors, and with spirit determined to support her just rights: though forsaken now in her distress by those allies, who owe their independency to her protection, she feared not in such a cause to stand alone against all the efforts of France; she sent forth her naval strength, but the enemy soon rendered the attempts of that ineffectual, by resolving never to try its force: In what manner was she now to employ it?—One only object remained worthy of its attention, and that was to destroy the trade of the enemy, and to intercept the succours which she sent to her dominions in America. Though this would not crush at once the evil, it would stop at least the sources that fed it, and might in the end contribute to induce the enemy to consent to a reasonable peace.

France endeavoured again to obviate this stroke by her policy. She took off the tax of 50 sous per ton, which she always chuses to keep on foreign freightage: she opened even her American ports, and admitted other countries into that choice part of her commerce, which, by her maritime regulations, she hath at other times so strictly reserved to herself. Neutral nations seized at once on the advantage, and opened to the enemy new channels for

for the conveyance of thofe riches, by which the war was to be nurfed and protracted: under the banner of friendfhip they thus ferved the caufe of the adverfary, whofe wealth fecured by that protection would have paffed fafe and unmolefted through our fleet; if Britain, again raifing her fpirit, had not refolved, that by this means her naval power fhould not be rendered ufelefs, and feized on the enemy's property, which fhe found on board neutral fhips.—It is well known, however, that her conduct in this refpect hath not been univerfally approved, and that fome neutral nations think they have a right to carry in their veffels unmolefted the property of our adverfaries.—As I here differ with them in fentiment, this is the point, on which I intend to difcourfe.

Great and wife governments have always been jealous of national glory: it is an active principle which, properly cultivated, operates in virtuous actions through every member of the ftate; to preferve this therefore in its purity is the duty of every one who loves his country.—Can it then be wondered, that the native of a kingdom, always celebrated for its public fpirit, and its upright faith, at a time when thefe are called in doubt, fhould
inte-

interest himself in its defence? No indecent charges shall here be urged against other countries, it is meant only to vindicate the honour of our own. It is to be lamented, that the necessity of affairs should at such a season have given occasion to this dispute, particularly with that ancient ally of England, who hath so often fought with her under the same banner, in support of the just rights and privileges of mankind: the zeal of any government to encourage the industry of its people, is what a British pen can never disapprove: the principle is noble, and merits even our applause; I only mean to shew, that the present object of it is not just.

I shall therefore examine the right, which neutral powers claim in this respect; first, according to the law of nations, that is, according to those principles of natural law, which are relative to the conduct of nations, such as are approved by the ablest writers, and practised by states the most refined.---I shall then consider the alterations, which have been made in this right by those treaties, which have been superadded to the law of nations, and which communities, for their mutual benefit, have established among themselves.

The

The right of protection then muft have its foundation in fome law, and, when confidered in relation to any particular cafe, it muft be founded on that law, by which the interefts of the parties concerned are generally determined, and which hath force in that place, where the right of protection is claimed. Thus in the prefent cafe, if neutral nations have any right to protect the property of the enemy, it muft take its rife from thofe laws, which are the eftablifhed rules of conduct between nations, and particularly on that element, where this right is fuppofed to be exerted. No civil or municipal inftitutions, and much lefs the privileges arifing from them, can here take place; they have no force but under the dominion of thofe who agreed to their eftablifhment. The queftion then is---How far, according to the law of nations, doth this right of protection extend?---To anfwer this clearly, we muft obferve, that governments can have fucceeded to no other rights, but fuch as their refpective members enjoyed in a ftate of individuality; and that one nation is now to another, as it were in a ftate of nature, that is, in the fame condition in which man was to man before they entered into fociety; the right therefore of protection, which individuals would have enjoyed

enjoyed in such a situation, is the same which government can claim at present :---An individual then in a state of nature, would have had an undoubted right to protect his own person and property against any attack ;---but if I am engaged in contention with another, would he then have had a right to protect him against me?---most certainly not ;---since he thereby would deprive me of a right, which the law of nature, for my own security, would in such a case give me, of seizing the property of this my enemy, and destroying his person : if he thought my conduct manifestly injurious, so as to call for general resentment, he would, on that account, become my enemy himself; but as long as he calls himself a neuter, to act in this manner against me would be no less absurd than unjust :—such therefore, and no more, is the right of protection, which governments enjoy at present in those places, to which their own dominions do not extend ; they have succeeded to the rights only of their respective members, and by consequence these alone they can protect.

But it will be asked,—From whence then arises the right, which governments alway enjoy, of protecting the property of the enemy within

within the precincts of their own country?—It is a confequence of the right of dominion; unlefs, therefore, their dominion extends over the ocean, the right of protection cannot there take place: dominion gives a right of enacting laws, of eftablifhing new jurifdictions, and of making all (whether its own fubjects or thofe of other countries) fubmit to thefe, who come within the pale of its power. Here then the trial, which the law of nations gives, is, as it were, fuperfeded; and any proceedings upon it would of courfe be unjuft; but as foon as you are out of the verge of this particular jurifdiction, the laws thereof and the privileges which attend them ceafe at once, and the general laws of nations again have their force: here the property even of an ally hath no other protection than what thefe laws allow it: being joined, therefore, to the goods of an enemy, it cannot communicate its protection to thefe, fince the fame law which gives fecurity to the firft, allows you to feize and deftroy the latter. Thefe reafonings are exemplified by a common fact; —within the precincts of the dominion of any government, you are not at liberty to fearch the fhips of any country; but is not this liberty univerfally and immemorially practifed over all on the main fea? and wherefore is this

this search made, but that, according to the law of nations, all are here answerable for what they may convey?

There is something analogous to this in most civil governments. Few countries are without some places which enjoy a right of protection from the general laws of the state, such as palaces, houses of religion, and the like; and this right generally arises from some pretence to an exclusive jurisdiction; as long, therefore, as any particular property remains within the verge of these, however justly it may be the object of the law, it is not subject to the power of it; but suppose it conveyed from hence into the public roads, beyond the precincts of this particular palace, or convent, the protection it received would vanish at once, and the general laws of the community would fully then have force upon it. Thus the protection which governments can give within their dominions extends not to the sea; the ocean is the public road of the universe; the law of which is the law of nations, and all that pass thereon, are subject to it without either privilege or exemption.

If this manner of reasoning should not clearly establish my point, I can appeal in
sup-

support of it to the ablest writers on public law, who will be found to have decided the question in my favour.

And first I will produce the testimony of that learned native of Delft, who wrote so nobly on the freedom of navigation to serve his ungrateful country. In one of the passages, which are now before me, it is remarkable, how much he labours to give the greatest extent to the rights of commerce; and yet with all his laudable bias to this favourite point, he is clearly of opinion, that the ship of a neutral nation cannot protect the property of an enemy: he manifestly implies,[*] that the vessels even of allies are subject to condemnation on account of the enemies property, with which they are laden; when it appears that this property was put on board them with the consent of the owners of the vessels, but not otherwise. His words are, " Neque amicorum naves in prædam veniunt ob res hostiles, nisi consensu " id factum sit dominorum navis ;" and producing several authorities in confirmation of this opinion, he afterwards adds, " Alioqui " res ipsæ solæ in prædam veniunt ;" but if

[*] Grotius de Jure Belli ac Pacis, lib. iii. c. 6. sec. 6. in notis.

the enemies property should be found laden on board a neutral vessel, without the connivance of the owner, in such case, "that "property alone is lawful prize:" and speaking again in another place on this point, he says, that if the wrong done me by my enemy is manifestly unjust, and that any one, by affording succours, should encourage him in his enmity against me, "jam non tantum ci- "viliter tenebitur de damno, sed & crimina- "liter, ut IS, qui judici imminenti reum "manifestum eximit."* A fine and animated manner of expression, which shews how clear the opinion of this great author was upon the question.

To the testimony of Grotius I shall add that of Bynkershoek, a native also of Holland, and whose sentiments, in point of maritime jurisprudence, Barbeyrac often prefers even to those of the former; and what makes even his opinion at this time of great importance, is, that he wrote principally for the use of the courts and states of the United Provinces, and generally confirms what he advances by their judgements and resolutions. He speaks expressly in favour of my point:

* Grotius de Jure Belli ac Pacis, lib. iii. cap. 1.

"Ra-

"Ratione consultâ," says he,* "non sum qui videam, cur non liceret capere res hostiles quamvis in navi amicâ repertas, id enim capio, quod hostium est, quodque jure belli victori cedit." He then assigns this reason also for his opinion, that as it is lawful to stop on the ocean any vessel, though she carry the colours of a neutral nation, and to examine by her papers to whom she really belongs, and in case she appear to be the property of an enemy, to seize her as a lawful prize; so he can see no cause why this rule should not extend to the effects which any ship may have on board; and if the goods of an enemy should lie there concealed, why they also, by the right of war, should not be taken and condemned: he even declares it to be his opinion, that the owner of the neutral vessel should, in such a case, lose the price of the freight; a severity which the English courts of admiralty never practise, where some particular circumstance doth not require it.

I shall add to these the opinion of Albericus Gentilis,†esteemed the ablest writer on national jurisprudence till Grotius bore the palm from

* Bynkershoek, Questionum Juris Publici, lib. i. cap. 14.
† Albericus Gentilis de Advocatione Hispanica, lib. 1. cap. 28.

him;

him; and his fame in this respect was so great, that Philip the Third of Spain appointed him perpetual advocate for his subjects in all causes, which they might have depending in the courts of England. This author states a case, where the Tuscans had taken the effects of the Turks, at that time their enemies, which they found on board some English ships; and he determines, that the Turkish goods are legal prize, but that the captor must pay the freight to the English. " Trans-" eunt res," says he, " cum suâ causâ, victor " succedit in locum victi, tenetur etruscus " pro toro naulo." The property of the enemy passeth to the captor, but all its consequences attend it; the goods justly belong to him, but he must pay to the freighter all which the enemy would have paid, to whose right he hath in every respect succeeded.

To enter particularly into the sentiments of any more writers on this subject would be equally tedious and unnecessary; it will be sufficient to mention the names alone of such others as are in favour of the question.— Among these I find Heineccius,* no less famed for his knowledge of laws, than for his

* Heineccius de Navibus ob Vecturam de Vetitarum Mercium commissis, cap. 2.

learn-

learning in what are the best expositors of laws, the antiquities of governments.— Zouch,* who for many years presided in the courts of admiralty of this kingdom.—Voet,† Zuarius,‡ and Loccenius,§ all of them writers of reputation, and whose opinions are universally relied on by all who treat on public jurisprudence.

I might indeed have wholly omitted the sentiments of these learned individuals, since we shall find, that great communities themselves have confirmed our opinion both by their laws and by their practice.—It will not be proper on this occasion to look far back into the early annals of the European states; when the governments of these were yet in their infancy, the advantages of commerce were but little understood, and of course the rights of it were not sufficiently regarded; war was then too much the season of rapine, and they who entered into it meant less to conquer than to plunder. As soon, however, as some better order began to be introduced into these affairs, it then became usual for each party at the com-

* Zouch de Judicio inter Gentes, pars 2.
† Voet de Jure Militari, cap. 5.
‡ Zuarius de Ulsu Maris, Consil. ii.
§ Loccenius de Jure Maritimo, lib. ii. cap. 4.

mencement of the war to publish a declaration, wherein he specified what kind of trade he would permit neutral nations to carry on with his enemy; and the regulations of these were sometimes attended to, and sometimes not, either as the interest of the party neutral inclined him to submit to the restraint, or as the power of the party belligerent enabled him to enforce the execution of it. True it is, that the prohibitions which these declarations contain are various, according to the sentiments of the different governments which made them; and on that account they are, perhaps, too unsteady a foundation on which to establish a right; there plainly, however, follows from hence one powerful inference in our favour, that not one can be found amid all this variety, which ever permitted neutral nations to protect the property of the enemy: this branch of freightage they all agree unanimously to prohibit.

The free states of Italy cultivated first the interests of commerce: before any vessel had as yet passed the Cape of Good Hope, and a shorter passage had been discovered to the East Indies, Venice and Genoa drove the principal trade of the world, and disperfed the manufactures of Asia to the different parts of Europe:

rope : it naturally followed, that these two commercial republics soonest understood and defined the just rights of navigation; their maritime constitutions still remain collected in the Consolato del Mare ; and the reputation of these was so great, that as the laws of Rhodes were once to the Romans, and the laws of Oleron to the western parts of Europe, so these Italian laws became of force universally to all nations which border on the Mediterranean sea: these have determined the point expressly in our favour. In one of them it is asserted, " Se la nave o navilio,
" che pigliato sarà, fusse di amici e le mer-
" cantie, che lui porterà saranno d'inimici, lo
" armiraglio della nave o del navilio armato,
" pou forzare & constringere quel patrone di
" quella nave o d'quel navilio, che lui pigliato
" haverà, che lui con quella sua nave gli debba
" portare, quello, che di suoi inimici sara;"
" If the ship or vessel which shall be taken
" belong to an ally, and the merchandize
" which she has on board belong to an ene-
" my, the captain of the armed ship may
" force or constrain the master of the ship or
" vessel which he has taken, to carry into
" some port for his account, the effects of his
" enemy which are on board;" and it is afterwards added, that the master of the vessel

D must

muſt be paid for the freightage of the goods of the enemy.*—And ſuch was not only the conſtant purport of their laws, but the practice of their governments was always conformable to it. Their hiſtorian † tells us, that in the war between the Venetians and the Genoeſe, the ſhips of Grecians, who were neuter, were always ſearched, and the enemies who lay hid in them were taken out and made priſoners.

It is unneceſſary to dwell longer in giving a further detail of the conduct of every nation in this reſpect; I will, therefore, confine myſelf to thoſe who are moſt concerned in the preſent diſpute; and will ſhew, that as England claims no more at preſent than what ſhe always enjoyed, ſo France and Holland have conſtantly ſupported the ſame opinion whenever their intereſt required it.

It was in the reign of the firſt Edward, a prince who thoroughly underſtood the rights of his crown, and had a ſpirit equal to the ſupport of them, that Philip the Fair of France, being engaged in a war with the Duke of Burgundy, the French admiral took

---

* Il Conſolato del Mare, c. 273.
† Nicep. Grogoras, lib. ix.

the ships of several neutral nations, which were passing through the British Channel into the ports of Flanders: great complaints were made on this head, and commissioners were appointed to examine into the conduct of the admiral; a libel was there presented against him by almost every trading nation of Europe; the record * of this is still remaining; and if neutral nations had at that time pretended to enjoy the right of protecting the property of the enemy, and that the effects which they carried on board their ships, could in no case, except in that of contraband, be made lawful prize, we might well expect, that this right would here have been claimed and asserted: fear could not, in this case, have prevented it; for all the world, except France, was on one side of the question; but the record contains no such claim: the injured demand their right on a different principle, because their ships were taken on those seas, " where the kings of England
" (saith the record) have time out of mind
" been in peaceable possession of the sovereign
" lordship, with power of appointing laws,
" of prohibiting the use of arms, of giving
" protection as occasion should require, and

* Sir Ed. Coke's Fourth Inst. chap. 22.

"appointing all things neceffary for the main-
"taining peace, juftice, and equity among
"all, as well foreigners as natives, who na-
"vigate thofe feas."* Here then the right of
protection is placed on that bafis, on which
alone it can properly be founded, the right of
dominion; no other pretence is offered; and
if I may be allowed to fum up the evidence,
as their names are written in the record,
"Genue, Cateloigne, Efpaigne, Alemaine,
"Seland, Hoyland, Frife, Denmarch, Nor-
"way, & plufours aultres lieux del Empier,"
all join here in afferting the principles on
which I firft eftablifhed my argument.

The annals of Edward III. afford ftill other
facts in favour of my opinion: this prince
added to his military accomplifhments, great
fagacity in the fcience of laws, and uncom-
mon attention to the commercial interefts of
his kingdom; in the fecond year of his reign
he confirmed the Charter of Privileges, which
fome of his predeceffors had before granted to
foreign merchants, and particularly to thofe
of the Hanfe-towns,† who were at that time
the greateft freighters of the Weftern parts of
Europe: this inftrument may well be confi-

---

* See all this more fully ftated in the record.
† Rymer's Fœdera, tom. 4. p. 361.

dered as a sort of maritime regulation, by which England meant to direct her conduct at that time in affairs of this nature: in this, liberty of navigation is fully confirmed; foreign merchants are allowed to carry their goods, whether purchased within the kingdom or without, " Quocunque voluerint;" but with this exception, " præterquam ad Terras no-
" toriorum & manifestorum hostium Regni
" nostri;"* and some offences being afterwards committed against this charter in the succeeding wars, it was again renewed in the same manner in the 6th year of this reign; in both these instances the exception is express, that no trade whatsoever should be permitted with the enemy; but this good king, perhaps through a principle of justice, and his ardent love to commerce, seems to have practised this right with more moderation, that is, in much the same manner in which the government of England claims it at present; for in his wars with Scotland, some ships of Great Yarmouth having taken several vessels belonging to the burgesses of the town of Bruges, " Prætendentes Bona in iisdem existentia
" fuisse hominum de Scotia," he directed his precepts to the Sheriff of Norfolk,† com-

* Rymer's Fœdera, tom. iv. p. 516.
† Ib. p. 328.

manding

manding him to fet at liberty, and to caufe full reftitution to be made of the fhips, and of fuch of the goods as belonged to the merchants of Bruges, and that he fhould detain only that part of the cargo which was the property of the Scotch, his enemies. We find alfo, that when Queen Elizabeth was engaged in war with Spain, fhe feized feveral veffels of the Hanfe-Towns, which were entering into the port of Lifbon; and fhe urged, among other arguments, the charter above mentioned in defence of her conduct: fhe was in this refpect fo fatisfied of the juftice of her caufe, that the threats of the German Empire, and other neutral powers, could not oblige her to relinquifh her right; and though fhe might perhaps on this occafion give too great extent to this right, yet it is remarkable that Monfieur de Thou, who was himfelf a great lawyer, and had long fat in the firft court of judicature in France, even when he blames the conduct of the Queen in this affair, paffeth his cenfure upon it, not as defective in juftice, but only in policy: " In tam alieno " tempore," fays he,* " Rerum prudentiores " exiftimabant, imprudenter factum effe a " Regina ab Anglis."

* Thuanus, lib. 96.

We

We have as yet mentioned the conduct alone of thofe Englifh princes, who knew how to affert their rights, and who ruled their people with glory; but we fhall find that even under a weaker government, and in a latter period, this right of feizing the property of the enemy found on board neutral fhips hath been fully claimed and practifed: when Villiers, Duke of Buckingham, prefided over the naval affairs of England, and to gratify his own private refentments, had engaged his country in a war againft Spain, the Britifh fleet under Pennington took feveral French veffels, to the number of between thirty and forty, which had Spanifh effects on board; they were brought into the ports of England, and our courts of admiralty condemned the goods of the Spaniards as legal prize, but ordered the veffels of the French to be releafed, and the freightage to be paid to them. This conduct was avowed by the Court of England, and a full reprefentation of it tranfmitted by the Lord High Admiral to the adminiftration of France: about 15 years after this, when the French themfelves were at war with Spain, the navy of France took a great many Englifh fhips which were laden with the property of Spaniards; and their courts of admiralty condemned not only the enemy's effects,

effects, but the English ships which conveyed them: the Earl of Leicester, then ambassador in France, made great complaints on this head; he was answered, that the English always acted in this manner; and this answer being transmitted to the Earl of Northumberland, at that time Lord High Admiral, he consulted upon it Sir Henry Martin, the best English civilian of that age, and the most versed in maritime jurisdiction; and by his advice he returned to Lord Leicester the following answer, which at the same time proves the constant opinion, and shews the moderation of the British Admiralty on this point: " that," says he,* " which is alledged by the French
" to be practised in our courts of admiralty
" is absolutely denied; and that neither the
" law nor practice hath ever been here to
" confiscate the goods of friends for having
" enemies goods among them: we are so far
" from doing any such act of injustice, as
" when in time of war we have met with
" any such prizes, the freight hath always
" been paid by the taker for those enemies
" goods that he took, and those that belonged
" unto friends were duly restored to them."

* The Sidney Papers, Algernon Earl of Northumberland to Robert, Earl of Leicester, Nov. 5, 1640.

Thus

Thus much may suffice to shew the conduct of the people of England:—history will also prove to us, that Holland hath always exerted the same right:—At the beginning almost of that war which the United Provinces sustained in support of their liberties, and even before their sovereignty was as yet fully established, the people of Zealand scrupled not to carry into their ports all such neutral vessels * as were conveying the effects of the enemy, under pretended names, from Flanders into Spain; and the courts of admiralty of that province adjudged the Spanish property to be legal prize; and though they released the neutral ships, they made them no compensation for their freightage: among these there were some English vessels, and Queen Elizabeth, angry that so young a state, and one which had placed itself under her protection, should in any degree interrupt the commerce of her people, at first shewed the effects of her resentment, by seizing their ships, and imprisoning their merchants; the Zealanders upon this made reprisals; several English vessels were detained, and their commanders put under confinement: to endea-

* Historia Belgica Metereni, lib. 5. Camden, anno 1575. Zouch de Judicio inter Gentes, pars 2.

vour at some settlement of this affair, the Queen sent over to Holland Mr. Robert Beal, her secretary; and for the same purpose the Prince of Orange dispatched a minister to London; by these means the dispute at last was compromised: the ships and the prisoners were on both sides released; but the Queen never obtained restitution of the enemies goods which were taken on board the vessels of her subjects; this fact is worthy of observation, not only as it relates to the conduct of Holland, but as it shews how far a Princess thought herself obliged in equity to yield, whom historians have always described as positive in her temper, and, whenever her right was concerned, of a very tenacious disposition.

Holland, whenever she was engaged in war, almost constantly pursued the same conduct: she sometimes even prohibited the commerce of neutral nations beyond all justice and moderation. In the year 1599,* when the government of Spain first prohibited the subjects of the United Provinces from trading to the ports of that kingdom, a liberty which had unaccountably been allowed them, from

* Grotii Hist. lib. 8.

the

the commencement of their revolt to that period; the States General, in revenge, publiſhed a placart, forbidding the people of all nations to carry any kind of merchandiſe into Spain; the words of Grotius, in the relation he has given of this affair in his Belgic Hiſtory, are very full and expreſs: " Per edic-
" tum," ſays he, " vetant populos quoſcun-
" que ullos commeatus refve alias in Hiſpa-
" niam ferre; ſi qui ſecus faxint, ut hoſti-
" bus faventes vice hoſtium futuros." This placart they publicly notified to all kings and nations, for this reaſon, as the hiſtorian expreſſes it, " ne quis inſcitiam excuſaret." The conſequences of this notification deſerve alſo our attention; the hiſtorian continues: " Paruit Rex Galliæ, ac ſi quis ſuo-
" rum ſex intra menſes in Hiſpaniam navi-
" gat, profeſſus eſt privatum periculum fore." Henry the Fourth, at that time king of France, though delivered then from all his diſtreſſes, and arrived at the ſummit of all his power, ſcrupled not to ſubmit to this placart, and gave up the intereſts of all his ſubjects, who ſhould attempt within ſix months to tranſgreſs it: the hiſtorian concludes, " Cæ-
" teri (reges) ſilentio tranſmiſere;" the other powers of Europe made no clamorous complaints againſt this meaſure of the States; in

silence they passed it over: How unlike was this conduct to that of Holland at present! —Charles the Second, in a letter to the States General, of October 4, 1666, charges them with a remarkable violence of this nature; being at war with some Asiatic Princes in the East Indies, they seized all the ships and goods of the English merchants which were trading to those countries; and the Dutch governors scrupled not only to profess in their declarations, " Qu' ayant depuis " peu annoncé la guerre aux Princes, avec qui " ils avoient dessein de trafiquer, cette guerre " devoit par consequent leur interdire tout " commerce avec les dits Princes."*

I omit citing many other instances of their conduct in this particular, lest I should appear tedious, especially as one fact still remains, which is alone sufficient to evince the opinion of Holland on this point; and the which I rather chuse to mention, as it happened even after the Dutch had by their negociations endeavoured to establish, as a general maxim among nations, that the goods of an enemy under a neutral banner should pass unmolested.—At the commencement of that war

---

* Charles the Second's Letter to the States General, October 4, 1666.

which broke out immediately after the revolution, when the firſt grand alliance was formed againſt France, Holland entered into a convention * with England to prohibit totally the commerce of neutral powers with the enemy: in the preamble of this, they aſſign publicly their reaſons for it; they ſay, " that " having declared war againſt the Moſt Chriſ- " tian King, it behoves them to do as much " damage as poſſible to the common enemy, " in order to bring him to agree to ſuch con- " ditions as may reſtore the repoſe of Chriſ- " tendom: and that for this end it was neceſ- " ſary to interrupt all trade and commerce " with the ſubjects of the ſaid king; and " that to effect this, they had ordered their " fleets to block up all the ports and havens " of France;" and afterwards, in the ſecond and third articles of this convention, it is agreed, " that they would take any veſſel, whatever " king or ſtate it may belong to, that ſhall " be found ſailing into or out of the ports of " France, and condemn both veſſel and mer- " chandiſe as legal prize; and that this reſo-, " lution ſhould be notified to all neutral " ſtates." Such therefore was at this time

* Convention concluded at London, Aug. 22, 1689.

the

the avowed opinion of Holland, and England was induced to join with her in this convention, exceeding thereby those bounds of equity and moderation, which she had almost always practised in this point before, and which she will, I hope, most faithfully observe for the future. The Northern Crowns, who were particularly affected by this prohibition, contended very vehemently against it: in answer to their objections were urged, the circumstances of affairs, the danger of Europe, and the mighty strength of that ambitious power; which, if some extraordinary effort was not made, would bring mankind under its subjection. It is remarkable, that Puffendorf,* who owed his fortune and employments to one of those Northern Crowns, was of opinion in this case against them, and thought that the convention might be justified. It is not meant here at present either to censure or commend it: circumstances may sometimes make a thing to be lawful, which considered by itself, would be unjust; but such times are truly unhappy, when necessity must be pleaded in support of a right.

---

* See a Letter of Puffendorf in Jno. Groningii Bibliotheca Universalis Librorum Juridicorum, p. 105.

It remains that I now inquire into the conduct of France; my proofs * on this head will be clear; they are indeed nothing lefs than the public laws of that kingdom; by fome very old French ordinances it is declared, not only that the enemies goods fhall be adjudged to be lawful prize, but that the neutral veffel which carries them, or the property of any ally which fhall be joined with them, fhall be joined alfo in the condemnation. It has always been a maxim of the courts of maritime jurifdiction of France, " Que la robe d'am con-
" fifque celle d'enemie:" and fo clear were they in this opinion, that the laws which eftablifhed it were repeatedly enacted in the reigns of two of their kings, Francis I. and Henry III.—That the practice of the French marine hath in this particular been conformable to their laws, may be proved by a thoufand inftances: I fhall felect one upon the authority of a Minifter of Holland, which will fhew what their conduct was in that Spanifh war which preceded the Pyrenean treaty. In a letter of Monfieur Boreel from Paris to Monfieur de Wit, December 26th, 1653 " On tient ici," fays he, " pour

* See the Ordinances of France, Francis I. 1543. c. 4. 2d Henry III. 1584. c. 69.

" maxi-

" maxime favorable à leurs interests, que
" leurs enemies ne doivent recevoir ni defenſe
" ni ſervice des ſubjects de leur H. H. P. P.
" en tranſportant de chez eux quelques mer-
" chandiſes ou commodités ou d'autres, qui
" ſeroient pour le compte de l'enemie, ſous
" peine, au cas qu'ils les trouvent dans les
" batiments Hollandois, qu'ils feront de bonne
" priſe, & qu'on les puiſſe enlever les dits ba-
" timents & les confiſquer."

But it is not the old laws of France alone, that thus determine this point, their more modern regulations confirm it: one of the laſt and greateſt ſervices which Colbert performed to his country, was the eſtabliſhment of a ſyſtem of naval laws, the wiſeſt and beſt digeſted which the ſpirit of legiſlation hath ever yet produced; it is obſervable, that although the ordinance which contained theſe laws was regiſtered in 1681, ſeveral years ſubſequent to thoſe treaties, by which France agreed that neutral veſſels ſhould protect the property of the enemy, yet it pays no attention to them, and eſtabliſhes the contrary doctrine. This proves how little regard France always ſhewed to that article. The words of the ordinance expreſsly condemn not only the enemies

mies goods, but the neutral ship which carries them: "All ships (saith the law*) which have goods on board that belong to the enemy, shall be good prize."

These laws continue still to be observed in France: at the commencement even of the present war, the French government delivered to Monf. Berkenrode, the Dutch minister at Paris, a memorial, " Contenant les Precautions," (as the title expresses it) " que doivent prendre les negociants Hollandois conforment à l'ordinance de la marine & aux reglements de la France, pour eviter que leurs navires soient declarés de bonne prise." In the preamble of this, the words of the above-mentioned law are repeated, and the same rule of condemnation is declared to be still in force: And the seventh article of the memorial lays even a greater restriction on neutral commerce, than the ordinance of 1681 seems to have intended; it is there said, " Si les navires Hollandois transportoient des merchandises du cru ou fabriques des enemies de la France, ces merchandises seroient de bonne prise, mais le corps du navire seroit relaché."—By this memorial, there-

---

* Naval Ordinance of 1681, Title ix. Art. 7.

fore, every thing which is either of the growth or manufacture of the enemy's country, when found on board the ships of Holland, though the property does not appear to belong to the enemy, is declared to be good prize. The same restriction evidently extends to all other neutral traders.* Is not this almost a total prohibition to neutral powers, of any commerce with the enemies of France?

Let us now look back on what has been said: the deduction which I have made hath, I fear, been tedious; but the importance of the subject by force led me into it:—I flatter myself, however, it has appeared, that reason, authority, and practice, all join to support the cause I defend:—by reason, I have endeavoured to trace out those principles on which this right of capture is grounded; and to give that weight to my own sentiments which of themselves they would not deserve, I have added the authorities of the ablest writers on this subject;—and lastly, I have entered largely into the conduct of nations, that I might not only lay thereby a broader foundation for this right, but that I might the more fully illustrate, by the extravagant pretensions

---

*. See the preamble of the Memorial.

of other states in this respect, the present moderation of England: no age or country ever gave a greater extent to the commerce of neutral nations, and we have seen that most in the same circumstances have confined it within much narrower bounds.

There remains still, however, one objection to what has been said, and that of so plausible a cast, that I cannot leave it without an answer: it has been pretended, that the liberty of navigation is destroyed by means of these captures, and that a violent restraint hath been put on the lawful industry of mankind. The liberty of navigation, in fair construction, can mean no more than the right of carrying to any mart unmolested the product of one's own country or labour, and bringing back the emoluments of it: but can it be lawful that you should extend this right to my detriment; and when it was meant only for your own advantage, that you should exert it in the cause of my enemy? Each man hath a right to perform certain actions, but if the destruction of another should follow from them, would not this be a just reason of restraint? The rights of mankind admit of different degrees, and whenever two of these come into competition, the lowest in the scale must always give

give place to the higher;—but you will say, that you have a profit in doing this; if, however, it is otherwise unjuft, will that confideration convert it into a right?—If you mean, that your own commerce ought to be free, that right is not in the leaft denied you; but if under this difguife you intend to convey freedom to the commerce of the enemy, what policy or what juftice can require it? What can neutral nations defire more, than to remain amid the ravages of war in the fame happy circumftances which the tranquillity of peace would have afforded them? But can any right from hence arife, that you fhould take occafion from the war itfelf to conftitute a new fpecies of traffic, which in peace you never enjoyed, and which the neceffity of one party is obliged to grant you, to the detriment, perhaps deftruction, of the other? If this right was admitted, it would become the intereft of all commercial ftates to promote diffenfion among their neighbours; the quarrels of others would be a harveft to themfelves; and from the contentions of others they would gather wealth and power.---But, after all, the rights of commerce are not the real caufe of this difpute: and liberty of navigation is only a fair pretence, which ambition hath thought fit to hold forth, to intereft the trading ftates

of

of the world in its caufe, and to draw down their indignation upon England; this is not the firft time that a deceit like this has been practifed: when the power of Spain was at its greateft height, and Elizabeth wifely contended againft the mighty defigns of Philip, the capture of fome veffels belonging to the Hanfe Towns gave occafion to a conteft of this nature: but they were the emiffaries of Philip that then blew up the flame, and pretending a love to commerce, promoted the ambitious projects of their mafter: the Queen of England publifhed an apology for her conduct, and this was anfwered in a virulent and abufive manner, not from any of the Hanfe Towns, but from Antwerp, a city under the dominion of Spain, and it feemed to be written (fays Thuanus) " per hominem Philippi " partibus addictum, non tam pro libertate " navigationis et in Germanorum caufâ de- " fendendâ, quam in Hifpanorum gratiam, " et ad Reginæ nomen profcindendum:" the interefts of commerce were the pretended caufe of this difpute, but the real caufe was the intereft of Philip; the pretended defign was to preferve the liberty of navigation, but the real end was to ferve the caufe of ambition, and to deftroy the government of England;— this cafe need not be compared with our own at prefent, the refemblance is too obvious.

Here

Here then we might rest our cause, if the law of nations was the only foundation on which this point could be argued; but the bands of equity have been found alone too weak to hold the nations of the world to their duty; their interest taught them to renew and confirm these by contracts among themselves, and frequently to add thereto certain mutual advantages, greater than what the law of nations singly would have allowed them: — let us consider therefore, what influence these may have in the present case;— whatever they are, I mean to give them all the force which reason or justice can require: if our ancestors have betrayed the interest of of their country in granting any privileges of this nature, we, who have succeeded to their rights, are bound to abide by their concessions; it is the happiness of great kingdoms, whose power is equal to the support of their own independency, to be able to act up to those principles, which necessity hath often forced little states unhappily to abandon; those scandalous maxims of policy, which have brought disgrace both on the name and the profession, took their rise from the conduct of the little principalities of Italy, when distressed by the successive invasions which France and Spain made upon them, they

they broke or conformed to their leagues, as their own fecurity obliged them; and their refined fhifts and evafions formed into fyftems by able doctors of their councils, have compofed that fcience, which the world hath called politics; a fcience of fraud and deceit, by which kingdoms are taught to be governed on principles, which individuals would be afhamed to profefs; as if there could be no morality among nations, and that mankind being formed into civil focieties, and collectively confidered, were fet free from all rules of honour and virtue: maxims like thefe I mean to avoid; to follow them would bring difhonour on my country.

It muft then be allowed, that there are articles in fome of our maritime treaties with other nations, which have ftipulated, that, " All which fhall be found on board the " veffels belonging to the fubjects of thofe " countries, fhall be accounted clear and free, " although the whole lading or any part thereof " fhall, by juft title of property, belong to " the enemies of Great Britain;" fuch an article is inferted in thofe maritime treaties, which Great Britain hath made with France*

* Treaty between Great Britain and France, 24th Feb. 1677.

and Holland :* it has indeed by some been supposed, that the subjects of the crown of Spain have a right to enjoy a privilege of the same nature; certain, however, it is, that no such article as that above mentioned, can be found in the maritime treaties between that country and Great Britain, and particularly in that of Madrid of 1667, which is the principle maritime treaty at present in force between the two kingdoms; but as a mistake in this respect may possibly have arisen from a false interpretation of two articles in the treaty of Madrid, which declare in general,* that " the " subjects of the two crowns respectively " shall have liberty to traffic throughout all " countries, cultivating peace, amity, or neu- " trality with either of them, and that the " said liberty shall in no wise be interrupted " by any hindrance or disturbance whatsoever, " by reason of any hostility which may be " between either of the said crowns and any " other kingdoms:" and as the liberty here stipulated, may be by some erroneously imagined to extend so far, as to grant a right to carry freely the effects of the enemy; it will be proper here to remove this error, and to

---

* Treaty between Great Britain and Holland, 1st Dec. 1764.

† Treaty of Madrid, 1677.

stop

stop a little to shew the true design and meaning of these articles. This explanation is at present more necessary, as it will tend to illustrate the true sense of other stipulations of precisely the same purport, which may be found in several of our commercial treaties, and particularly in the first and second articles of that with Holland of Dec. 11, 1674: a wrong interpretation of which hath already given occasion to great confusion and much false reasoning upon the present question.

It cannot, I think, be doubted, that according to those principles of natural equity, which constitute the law of nations, the people of every country must always have a right to trade in general, to the ports of any state, though it may happen to be engaged in war with another, provided it be with their own merchandise, or on their own account; and that under this pretence, they do not attempt to screen from one party the effects of the other; and on condition also, that they carry not to either of them any implements of war, or whatever else, according to the nature of their respective situations, or the circumstances of the case, may be necessary to them for their defence. As clear as this point may be, it has sufficiently appeared by the facts deduced

duced above, that amid the regularities of war, the rules of equity in this refpect were not always enough regarded; and that many governments in time of war have often moft licentioufly difturbed, and fometimes prohibited totally, the commerce of neutral nations with their enemies: about the middle therefore of the laft century, when the commercial regulations, which at prefent fubfift between the European powers, firft began to be formed, it became abfolutely neceffary to call back the attention of governments to thofe principles of natural right, from whence they had ftrayed; and to fix and determine what was the law of nations, by the articles of their refpective treaties: for this purpofe, the negociators of that age inferted in their commercial regulations, articles * to the fame purport as thofe above-mentioned, afferting, in general, a right to trade unmolefted with the enemies of each other; and thefe they ufually placed among thofe articles of general import, which are commonly firft laid down in treaties, as the bafis on which the fubfe-

---

* Treaty of Commerce between France and Holland, 1662.—Treaty of Commerce between England and Holland, Feb. 17, 1668.—Treaty of Commerce between England and Holland, Dec. 1, 1674.—Treaty of Commerce between England and France, Feb. 24, 1677.

quent

quent ſtipulations are founded: the rule therefore of equity in this caſe being thus defined, they came afterwards to erect upon it ſuch privileges as that rule alone would not have allowed them; and among the reſt, ſome nations, as their intereſt prompted them, granted mutually to each other, by new and expreſs articles, the right of carrying freely the property of their reſpective enemies. Theſe laſt articles therefore muſt be conſidered as wholly diſtinct in their nature from thoſe before-mentioned, and in their meaning totally different: the firſt are an affirmance of an old rule, the laſt create a new privilege; thoſe only confirm a right which was determined by the law of nations before; theſe make an exception to that law:—if they both imply the ſame ſenſe, why are both ſo often found inſerted in the ſame * treaties? Would the repetition in ſuch a caſe have been neceſſary; and to what purpoſe were new articles added to grant a privilege which was already included in the terms of the preceding? The ſame exception alſo of contraband goods is again repeated in the laſt caſe, as well as in the former; and ſhews clearly,

---

* See the Treaties mentioned in the laſt note.

that the property, which is the object of the exception in the different articles, muſt likewiſe in its nature be different; the one relates to the ordinary means of traffic which every nation enjoys, its own produce or property; the other to the property of the enemy.

But this point is ſtill more clearly explained by the aſſiſtance of other treaties, where articles of the ſame force, as the 21ſt and 22d of the treaty of Madrid, are inſerted, and the intention of them fully made appear from the ſubſequent parts of the ſame treaties.—In the treaty of commerce between Great Britain and Sweden, of the 21ſt of October, 1661, it is ſtipulated by the 11th article, that " it is by " no means to be underſtood, that the ſub- " jects of one confederate, who is not a party " in a war, ſhall be reſtrained in their liberty " of trade and navigation with the enemies " of the other confederate, who is involved " in ſuch war;" and then in the article which immediately follows, the meaning of theſe words become manifeſt beyond a doubt: it is there ſo far from being ſuppoſed, that the liberty here granted can be ſo interpreted, as to imply a right of conveying the effects of an enemy, that the very attempt to

practiſe

practife it under favour of this liberty, is there called " a fraud;"* and as a " moſt heinous crime," is ordered " to be moſt feverely puniſhed;" and to prevent any collufion in this refpect, the veſſels of both parties are required to be furniſhed with paſſports, " fpecifying " of what nation the proprietors are to whom " the effects on board them belong."—And in the treaty of commerce between Great Britain and Denmark, of the 11th of July, 1670, a right of free trade with the enemy is ſtipulated in the 16th article; and afterwards by the 20th article, the extent of this right is made apparent: here the means are ſet down to prevent the defigns of thofe, who under favour of this ſtipulation ſhould attempt to protect the effects of the enemy; and the illegality of fuch a practice being fuppofed, as not neceſſary to be expreſſed, the article then declares, " but left this " liberty of navigation and paſſage for one " ally might, during a war which the other " may be engaged in, by fea or land, with " any other ſtate, be of prejudice to fuch " other ally; and the goods belonging to the " enemy be fraudulently concealed, under the " colourable pretence of their being in amity

* See the Treaty of Commerce between Great Britain and Sweden, Oct. 21, 1661.

" to-

" together; to prevent, therefore, all fraud of
" that fort, all ſhips ſhall be furniſhed with
" paſſports;" the form of which is there ſet down, and is the ſame as that mentioned above.—From theſe treaties then it manifeſtly appears, that by a general ſtipulation in favour of trade with the enemy of another power, negociators never intended to imply a right to carry freely the effects of that enemy; but that to eſtabliſh ſuch a right, it is neceſſary to have it expreſsly mentioned. The 21ſt and 22d articles therefore of the treaty of Madrid, in which liberty of traffic to the countries of the enemies of Great Britain is thus in general ſtipulated, can be explained to grant to the ſubjects of the Crown of Spain no other right but that of carrying on without any injuries, " moleſtation," or " diſturbance," ſuch traffic as would otherwiſe be legal according to the law of nations, and by this law, in time of war, it never could be legal to protect the effects of an enemy;—a privilege, however, like this Great Britain hath conſented to grant in her commercial treaties with France and Holland; the firſt of theſe is put an end to by the preſent war; it remains, therefore, that I now diſcourſe on this privilege, as it is ſtipulated in the Britiſh treaties with Holland; and I pro-

propose to shew that here also it is extinct.—
But to give a fuller view of my subject, and
to shew the origin and intention of this privilege, it will be necessary to enter a little into
the history of it, and to relate the manner in
which the article that grants it was first admitted into treaties.

When the United Provinces had put an end
by the treaty of Munster, to that long war,
which they had so nobly maintained in support of their liberties, and had happily crowned
their labours by obtaining a full acknowledge-
ment of their sovereignty; delivered from
the cares of war, they wisely turned their
thoughts towards the arts of peace : after long
contentions among themselves, their commercial provinces had at length obtained the
greatest lead in the state; the interest of trade
was of course the principal object of their
council; their armies were reduced; all who
favoured war were no longer in credit; and
the views of their ministers terminated chiefly
in giving permanence to that extensive traffic,
which had supported them through all their
distresses, and to the effects of which they
principally attributed all their power and freedom.

They

They were, indeed, at this time so fully masters of almost all the commerce of the world, that they had little else to do but to preserve the possession of it: the public was, on this occasion, amused with a new species of policy, the offspring rather of avarice than ambition, desirous of keeping the rest of mankind in indolence, that it might more fully reap the fruits of its own industry: where wealth was at least the first object in view, though in the end it might be accompanied by its usual attendant, power: the arts which they practised to preserve their fisheries, and to secure to themselves alone the trade of the Asiatic spices, are well known, and not at present to our purpose; they urged loudly the freedom of navigation, till they had made it free indeed for themselves; but they have been charged with practising a different doctrine on the other side of the line to what they professed on this; and with seeking to establish an exclusive trade on those very seas, whose freedom from papal grants and Spanish pretensions the pen of their Grotius had so ably defended.

There was, however, another species of commerce which demanded their attention, even more than either of the former; as it was

was not only a profitable branch of traffic in
itfelf, but as it greatly tended to the fecurity
of the reft, by being the principal bafis of
their naval power: this was the trade of
freightage, or the carrying trade, the fubject
of our prefent difcourfe.—To underftand their
views in this refpect, we muft firft take no-
tice of the foundation on which their policy
was built; they had fucceeded to the Han-
featic traders, in becoming the carriers of the
world: long poffeffion had, therefore, fur-
nifhed them with great numbers of failors
and fhips; and to thefe they added uncom-
mon parfimony and induftry, the natural en-
dowments of their people: thefe made them
contented with fmall profits, and enabled them
to carry the manufactures of each country
even cheaper than the natives of it themfelves: with fuch happy circumftances in
their favour, they were fure of making this
branch of trade wholly and perpetually their
own, if they could, by their negociations and
policy, eftablifh two points:—The firft was,
that no nation fhould grant to its own natives any privileges in relation to freightage, which the people of Holland fhould not
equally enjoy. And as the confequences of
war fhould otherwife frequently interrupt the
the courfe of this traffic, they laboured to obtain

tain, as their second point, that whenever any other nation was engaged in war, they might then enjoy, as neuters, the right of protecting the property of its enemies. These points, once obtained, would open a larger field, on which their industry might exert itself, than what they could otherwise of right pretend to enjoy: they were wise, however, in endeavouring to obtain it: no nation besides themselves had more shipping than what was equal to the carriage of their own manufactures! they alone, therefore, could carry on the freightage of other countries, and largely reap, when their neighbours were at war, the advantages proposed.

The regency of Holland laboured with great perseverance for the establishment of these two points: their great minister De Witt* filled all instructions and dispatches with every argument and motive which his active mind could invent in support of these favourite maxims: they were willing to give up any temporary advantage to gain that, which, once acquired, would prove for ages an overflowing spring of wealth. By their negociations they earnestly laboured to induce France

* Lettres de Monf. De Witt, passim.

to comply with their defires in thefe refpects;
but here they were a long while unfuccefsful:
in oppofition to the firft point of their policy, Fouquet, while he was at the head of
the French marine and finances, eftablifhed
the tax of 50 fous per ton on all foreign
fhipping; and endeavoured thereby to encourage and augment the freightage of his
own country; and when, upon his difgrace,
Colbert fucceeded to his employments, this
tax of 50 fous was almoft the only part of
the former's policy which the latter thought
fit to adopt. It is amazing, with what zeal
and application the minifters of Holland contended for the abolition of it: France at
length relaxed her feverity on this head, not
fo much to favour the trade of the Dutch,
as in compliance with the interefts of her
own. Colbert's great fchemes to improve the
manufactures of his country had met with
better fuccefs than his plans for the augmentation of its marine; and the frequent
wars in which his ambitious mafter involved
his kingdoms gave repeated checks to the
freightage of his people. France, therefore,
at laft found it neceffary to give a larger vent
to her manufactures, by opening her ports to
foreign veffels; and for this purpofe fhe took
off the tax of 50 fous, by the treaty of Ryf-
wick,

wick, as far as it related to the ships of Holland alone: and since that time she has regulated her conduct in this particular as the interest of her trade requires. In time of war, she always remits this tax, as she is then forced to make use of the freightage of neutral nations, her naval power not being equal to the protection of her own: and in time of peace she preserves the tax, or not, as the increase or diminution of her shipping requires, always giving the greatest encouragement to her own marine, which is consistent with the preservation of her manufactures.

France consented sooner to the other point of Dutch policy, and granted by treaty to the vessels of Holland, as neuters, the right of protecting the effects of an enemy: the laws of France, indeed, have continued always to determine against this right; and in this respect, therefore, their laws and treaties contradict each other: some very ancient ordinances of that kingdom (as we have shewn above) had adjudged as lawful prize in this case, not only the enemies goods, but had joined also in the condemnation the neutral vessel which carried them; the last, however, of these points was remitted as early as 1646, by a temporary treaty then made with Holland;

land; the neutral veffel, and all the effects of a friend found on board it, by this were ordered to be fpared: by a fubfequent negociation, Holland endeavoured to get this privilege farther confirmed and extended: it was one great part of Monfieur Boreel's employment in his long embaffy at Paris: at laft, however, in the memorable treaty of defenfive alliance between Holland and France, of the 27th of April, 1662, this favour was obtained in its full extent; by the 35th article* it is reciprocally agreed, that all which fhall be found on board the veffels of either of the contracting parties, " encore que la charge " ou partie d'icelle fut aux enemies, fera libre " & affranchie." This article was again renewed by the marine treaty of 1678, and by feveral fubfequent treaties: the marine treaty of December 21, 1739, was the laft in which it was inferted: this continued in force during part of the laft war; but in the year 1745 the French Government declared this treaty void by an act of council, and it hath never fince been renewed: France, from the condition of her marine, could certainly reap no advantage from the infertion of this article in her own treaties; but it was wife

---

* See the treaties in the Letters of D'Eftrade, tom. i.

in her to endeavour to eſtabliſh the point as a general maxim of national law among other countries; experience hath proved to her the uſe of it in time of war.

But Holland moſt exerted her policy to bring that nation to a compliance with her maxims, whom ſhe moſt apprehended as her rival in trade: the ſcandalous ignorance of the Engliſh miniſters in point of commerce, and the little attention which they paid to the intereſts of it, gave ſuch advantages for ſome time to the Dutch, that more veſſels of that country were ſeen in the ports of our colonies than even of our own; the ſhipping of England, from the reign of Elizabeth, had been in a conſtant decline; we ſhould hardly have believed, that in the reign of Charles I. England could not have furniſhed more than three merchant veſſels of 300 tons, if Sir Joſiah Child had not affirmed it: the time at length arrived, when we were to be put in this reſpect on an equality with our neighbours, and to vindicate (as it were) the advantages of our own induſtry and produce to ourſelves; in 1651, the Parliament of England paſſed into an ordinance that noble ſtrain of commercial policy, called ſince, the act of navigation; Mr. St. John returning about this

this time from his embaſſy at the Hague, became the happy inſtrument, which Providence made uſe of, to accompliſh this great work;* reſenting highly the refuſal, which had there been given to his propoſals, and the inſults which had been offered to his perſon, he warmly ſolicited, and at length induced the council of ſtate, to move the parliament to paſs it; the committee ſat five days in forming it; and it was at laſt publiſhed by order of the houſe with great pomp and ceremony at the Royal Exchange; the Dutch were ſo ſenſible of its conſequences, that it was the principal cauſe of the enſuing war: they called it in a manifeſto,† publiſhed ſoon after, " A vile act and order." At the negociations for that peace which put an end to the war, De Witt laboured with his uſual induſtry and acuteneſs to procure the abolition of it; his efforts were happily in vain; they who made the law attended with vigour the execution of it; the effects of it were immedialy apparent. This act of policy alone hath fortunately outweighed all our other follies and extravagancies; though condemned by ſome of our hiſtorians, and unnoticed by others, it hath proved the fertile ſource of all our naval

* Ludlow's Memoirs, vol. i. p. 345.
† The manifeſto of Holland, 1652.

power:

power: it hath operated infenfibly to our prefervation, and hath been the fpring from whence hath flowed the wealth and greatnefs of England.

Our anceftors, with equal conftancy, for fome time withftood the other maxim of Dutch policy, and would not permit their veffels, as neuters, to protect the effects of the enemy. By a very ancient and remarkable treaty, made when the dukes of Burgundy were fovereigns of the Low Countries, the contrary opinion had long been eftablifhed; in that it was determined, " Quod fubditi Unius Prin- " cipum Prædictorum," (that is, Henry VII. King of England, and Philip, Duke of Burgundy) " non adducent aut adduci facient " per mare, fraudulofe, vel quocunque co- " lore, aliqua bona feu merchandizas inimi- " corum alterius eorundem principum." And it farther ftipulated, that in cafe the mafter of the neutral veffel fhall endeavour, by a falfe report, to defraud the captor of any of his enemy's effects, he fhall be obliged to make good the lofs fuftained thereby, by the forfeiture of as much of his own. Frequent applications were made before the reftoration, both to the parliament and to the protector, to alter the courfe of proceeding in this refpect;

spect; but those heads which formed the act of navigation were too wise to consent to this; a particular occasion, however, at last induced England to make the concession; by the treaty of commerce made at the Hague, 17th of February, 1668, this point was fully settled to the satisfaction of Holland; by the 10th article * of which it was fully stipulated, that the shipping of each country should carry freely the goods of the enemies of the other. The circumstances of the time, and the situation of affairs when this article was framed, account for its admission into this treaty, and very strongly apologise for the authors of it; Lewis the XIVth had then just commenced the first career of his ambition, and England resolved with spirit to throw herself in his way. Holland was then engaged in a strong defensive alliance with France, from whom it was necessary to separate her, and to make her join with England to support the independency of Europe. The Dutch ministers seized this fortunate opportunity of obtaining from England the same advantages which they had already acquired by their treaties with France. It hath 'been the policy of most republics never to

* Intercursus Magnus in Rymer's Fœdera, vol. xii. p. 585.

enter into any alliance where some benefit doth not accrue to themselves; and Holland could not be expected to deviate from this maxim on the present occasion, in compliment to the king of England, who had always shewn but little affection to the States; the war also with that monarch was but lately ended, and the wound but weakly healed: the French treaty of 1662, besides its defensive stipulations, contained also several commercial regulations, the favourite object of Holland; these had been provisionally referred to a few months before at Breda, with a design to prevent any intermediate disputes between England and Holland, until a treaty of commerce, which was then under deliberation, was concluded; but unless these were perpetuated on the present occasion, and formed into a permament national treaty, to which England was averse,* the States were resolved not to join in the alliance proposed: Monf. De Witt expressly told Sir William Temple,† " That the treaty of defensive al-
" liance must, for a basis, have at the same
" time an adjustment of matters of com-
" merce;" and unless this could be obtained,

* Sir William Temple to Lord Arlington, Feb. 12, 1668.
† Ib. Jan. 24, 1668.

it was the avowed opinion of that great penfionary not to conclude. Influenced by the fentiments of their minifter, the States perfifted in the fame refolution; they forced, at laft, Sir William Temple to yield the point; apprehenfive of the leaft delay, and of the uncertainties which would neceffarily follow from it, he ventured to comply with their defires, though he exceeded thereby his inftructions; a private promife paffed firft between him and Monf. De Witt, and in confequence of that, a few weeks after, a treaty of commerce was concluded.

We have before obferved, that in the 35th article of the treaty of 1662, the French confented to grant the right of protection to neutral veffels; this, therefore, came of courfe to be inferted in our commercial treaty of 1668, and the advantages which would arife from thence in favour of the trade of Holland, were the conceffions which England then chofe to make, that fhe might obtain the affiftance of that republic againft France. To what other purpofe could England at this time eftablifh a rule of commerce, which fhe had before fo often refufed, and now fo reluctantly granted to the earneft folicitations of the States? Any benefit which the Britifh trade might reap from the mutual ſtipulation of this article, could never be the object which the miniſters of this country had in view. The article, conſidered by itſelf, is of the moſt fatal conſequence to the power and trade of Great Britain; when ſhe is at peace, and her neighbours are at war, ſhe cannot reap any benefit from it, as her own ſhipping is not more than equal to the trade of her people; and when, on the other hand, Great Britain is at war, and her neighbours at peace, it tends to defeat the beſt part of her power, and to render fruitleſs the efforts of her naval force; while at the ſame time, conſidered as a general maxim of right among other nations, Great Britain neither wants the uſe of it, as ſhe is equal in time of war to the protection of her own ſhipping; neither can her merchants enjoy the advantage of it, as the employment of foreign freightage is in moſt reſpects directly contrary to her laws. This article was again renewed in the treaty of commerce 1674, in conſequence of its having been before ſtipulated in that of 1668. The treaty of 1674 is the maritime regulation that at preſent ſubſiſts between Great Britain and Holland.

'In

In this manner, therefore, the article having obtained existence in these treaties, we are now to consider whether it is still in force.

Treaties of alliance being nothing more than stipulations of mutual advantages between two communities in favour of each other, ought to be considered in the nature of a bargain; the conditions of which are always supposed to be equal, at least in the opinion of those who make it; he, therefore, who breaks his part of the contract, destroys the equality or justice of it, and forfeits all pretence to those benefits, which the other party had stipulated in his favour: " Si pars " una" (says Grotius) * Fœdus violaverit, " poterit altera a Fœdere discedere, nam Ca- " pita Fœderis singula conditionis vim ha- " bent." And Puffendorf,† speaking of conventions, says, " Nec hæc alterum obli- " gant, ubi ab uno legibus conventionis non " fuerit satisfactum."

The next question then is—Hath Holland complied with her part of the treaties or con-

---

* Grotius de Jure Belli ac Pacis, lib. ii. cap. xv. sec. 15.
† Puffendorf de Jure Nat. & Gentium, lib. iii. cap. viii. sec. 8.

tracts, to which she is mutually bound with England?—Hath she performed all that she hath stipulated in our favour?—Or hath she been deficient in the execution of some article in which the very life of our alliance is contained?—If so material a part should be extinguished, it would be unnatural to suppose, that any lesser limb of the treaties should have vigour. Holland, in this case, could have no pretence to require the execucution of what may have been conceded in her favour; especially, if the performance of it would operate to the detriment of that ally whose friendship she hath forsaken.

I doubt not but my reader hath already answered in his own mind the question proposed—that the possessions of the crown of Great Britain in Europe have been attacked by the armies of France—that in consequence of this, on the 2d of August, 1756, the British government made to the States General in proper form the necessary requisition—that in such case Holland is obliged by treaties to grant immediate succours, and after a certain time to join with Great Britain in open war—that she hath not performed these conditions, and hath therefore forfeited all title to any advantages contained in those
                                                    treaties,

treaties, and above all, to such as may arise from the nature of the war itself?

I shall state, however, this point something more particularly; Holland is engaged in three different guaranties or defensive treaties with Great Britain: the first is that ancient original defensive alliance, which hath been the basis of all the subsequent treaties between the two nations: this treaty was designed to have been made immediately after the triple alliance, but the unsteady conduct of the ministers of Charles the Second, and the unfortunate attachment of that monarch to the French court, for some years delayed it: it was at last, however, concluded at Westminster the 3d of March, 1678: it is (except in two immaterial alterations) an exact copy of the twelve first articles of the French treaty of 1662; and both were negociated by the same minister, Monsieur Van Beuningen. In the preamble of this treaty, "the preservation of each other's dominions" is set forth as the cause of making it; and the stipulations of it are, " a mutual guaranty of " all they already enjoyed, or might hereafter " acquire by treaties of peace, in Europe " only." They farther guaranty, " all trea- " ties which were at that time made, or
" might

"might hereafter conjointly be made with
"any other power." They promife alfo,
"to defend and preferve each other in the
"poffeffion of all towns or fortreffes, which
"did at that time belong, or fhall for the fu-
"ture belong, to either of them;" and for
this purpofe it is determined, that "when
"either nation is attacked or molefted, the
"other fhall immediately fuccour it with a
"certain number of troops and men of war,
"and fhall be obliged to break with the ag-
"greffor in two months, immediately after
"the party that is already at war fhall re-
"quire it; and that they fhall then act con-
"jointly with all their forces, to bring the
"common enemy to a reafonable accommo-
"dation."

That Holland hath not complied with the terms of this guaranty is evident;—Minorca, "a poffeffion of the crown of Great Britain, "and which fhe acquired by treaty," hath been attacked: this is one cafe of the guaranty; by that attack, "a treaty that was "made in common concert," the treaty of Utrecht hath been broken; this is a fecond cafe of the guaranty; and by thefe means "England hath been deprived of a poffeffion "which of right belonged to her:" this is a third

third cafe of the guaranty; and notwithftanding all this, Holland hath not as yet granted the fuccours ftipulated; and many more than two months have paffed without her having entered into war conjointly with England, as the treaty requires.

The fecond fpecies of defenfive alliance which fubfifts between Great Britain and Holland, is that which was firft agreed to, in the treaty of barrier and fucceffion of October the 29th, 1709, and again more particularly ftipulated in another treaty to the fame purpofe of January 29th, 1713: the defign of this treaty is the guaranty of the Dutch barrier on one part, and the guaranty of the firmeft barrier of Britifh liberty, the Proteftant fucceffion, on the other: the ftipulations are,* " that in cafe either fhould be at-
" tacked, the other fhould furnifh at the re-
" quifition of the party injured, but at his
" own expence, certain fuccours there ex-
" preffed; and if the danger fhould be fuch
" as to require a greater force, that he fhall be
" obliged to augment his fuccours, and ulti-
" mately to act with all his power in open
" war againft the aggreffor." I pretend not

* Article xiv. of the treaty of Barrier and Succeffion of January 29, 1713.

to make any ufe of this treaty in the prefent cafe; and only mention it to give a fuller view of the alliances which fubfift between us. Here, however, I will indulge a wifh, that the cafe of this guaranty, as far as it relates to the right of the crown of Great Britain, may never again exift. I always read with forrow, that there ever was a time when the unfortunate diffenfions of our people, in a point where the whole of their happinefs was concerned, fhould have made it neceffary to add any other fanction to our own laws, than fuch as our own power can afford them. Thefe days, however, of fhame now, I hope, are paffed; more than forty years experience of the mildeft government muft have won the moft obdurate heart to confefs the prefent felicity, and blefs the hand which beftows it. When, forgetting ancient errors, we are thus united in defence, the affections of his Majefty's fubjects are the happieft guaranty of his right.

I come now to the laft fpecies of defenfive alliance which fubfifts between Great Britain and Holland. This was concluded at the Hague the 4th of January, 1717. To this treaty France was a party. The intention or view of it was, " the prefervation of each
" other

" other reciprocally in the poſſeſſion of their
" dominions, as eſtabliſhed by the treaty of
" Utretcht;" and the ſtipulations are, " to
" defend all and each of the articles of the
" ſaid treaty, as far as they relate to the con-
" tracting parties reſpectively, or each of
" them in particular; and they guaranty all
" the kingdoms, provinces, ſtates, rights,
" and advantages, which each of the parties
" at the ſigning of that treaty poſſeſſed:" and
in a ſeparate article all this is confined to
" Europe only." The ſuccours ſtipulated in
ſupport of this guaranty, are much the ſame
as thoſe mentioned above ; firſt, " interpoſi-
" tion of good offices,"—then, " a certain
" number of forces,"—and laſtly, " decla-
" ration of war." This treaty was renewed
by the quadruple alliance of 1718, and again
by the acceſſion of Holland to the treaty of
Hanover of 1726, and laſt of all by the 3d article of the treaty of Aix-la-Chapelle, 1748.

Holland hath by no means executed the
terms of this guaranty,—Minorca, " a poſ-
" ſeſſion of the crown of England in Europe,
" which ſhe enjoyed at the ſigning of this
" treaty," hath been attacked ; this is one
caſe of the guaranty. By this attack, " the
" article of the treaty of Utrecht, by which
" that

" that poffeffion was ceded to England,"
hath been broken ; this is another cafe of
guaranty. I need not again obferve, that
Holland, in confequence of this, hath neither
granted the fuccours, nor declared war, as this
treaty alfo requires.

It will, however, perhaps be objected, "that
" Great Britain was the aggreffor in the pre-
" fent war, and unlefs fhe had been firft at-
" tacked, the cafe of the guaranties doth not
" exift." True it is, that the treaties which
contain thefe guaranties, are called defenfive
treaties only ; but the words of them, and
particularly of that of 1678, which is the
bafis of all the reft, by no means exprefs the
point clearly in the fenfe of the objection ;
they guaranty in general " all the rights and
" poffeffions" of both parties, againft " all
" kings, princes, republics, and ftates ;" fo
that if either " fhall be attacked" or " mo-
" lefted," whether it be " by hoftile act or
" open war," or " in any other manner
" whatfoever, difturbed in the poffeffion of
" his eftates, territories, rights, immuni-
" ties, and freedom of commerce ;" it then
declares what fhall be done in defence of thefe
objects of the guaranty, by the ally, who is
not at war; but it is no where mentioned, as

neceffary.

necessary, that the attack of these should be the first injury or attack. Nor doth this loose manner of expression appear to have been an omission or inaccuracy. They who have framed these guaranties, certainly chose to leave this question without any farther explanation, to that good faith which must ultimately decide upon the execution of all contracts made between sovereign states. It is not presumed they hereby meant, that either party should be obliged to support every act of violence or injustice which his ally might be prompted to commit through views of interest or ambition. But, on the other hand, they were cautious of affording too frequent opportunities to pretend, that the case of the guaranties did not exist, and of eluding thereby the principal intention of the alliance; both these inconveniencies were equally to be avoided; and they wisely thought fit to guard against the latter of these, no less than the former. They knew that in every war between civilized nations, each party always endeavours to throw upon the other, the odium and guilt of the first act of provocation and aggression, and that the worst of causes was never without its excuse. They foresaw that this alone would unavoidably give sufficient occasion to endless cavils and disputes,
whenever

whenever the infidelity of an ally inclined him to avail himself of them. To have confined therefore the cafe of the guaranty, by a more minute defcription of it, and under clofer reftrictions of form, would have fubjected to ftill greater uncertainty, a point, which, from the nature of the thing itfelf, was already too liable to doubt; they were fenfible, that the cafes would be infinitely various, that the motives to felf-defence, though evidently juft, might not always be univerfally apparent; that an artful enemy might difguife the moft alarming preparations, and that an injured nation might be neceffitated to commit even a preventive hoftility, before the danger which caufed it could be publicly known. Upon fuch confiderations thefe negociators wifely thought proper to give the greateft latitude to this queftion, and to leave it open to a fair and liberal conftruction; fuch as might be expected from friends, whofe interefts thefe treaties were fuppofed to have for ever united, and fuch on the prefent occafion Great Britain hath a right to demand.

If, however, we fhould, for the prefent, wave this interpretation, and allow the treaties to have all the meaning, which they who make this objection require, the evidence
of

of facts will sufficiently prove, that France was the aggressor in the present war. If we look to America, the present war there is little more than a continuation of the last; repeated usurpations of the possessions of Great Britain have been there the constant employment of France, almost from the hour in which the treaty of Aix was signed; and these were at last followed by an avowed military attack upon a fort belonging to the crown of Great Britain, by regular troops, acting under a commission from the court of France. If we consider America as having no concern in the present question, the same ambitious power will also be found to have been the aggressor in the European war; France early manifested her hostile intentions in Europe; in 1753, in direct opposition to the express stipulations * of three solemn treaties she began to restore the port of Dunkirk; and Holland then considered this action in such a light as induced her, in conjunction with the British government, to present a memorial against it. France also gave another proof of her hostile intentions by her design to invade Great Britain, avowed by her ministers in every court in Eu-

* Ninth article of the treaty of Utrecht; fourth article of the treaty of the Hague, 1717; and seventeenth article of the treaty of Aix-la-Chapelle.

rope, and sufficiently manifested by the preparations which she publicly made for it. And these were likewise followed by an open attack upon an European island belonging to Great Britain, an attack upon the island of Minorca. It seems, indeed, allowed, by the opinion of the parties concerned, that by the attack of Minorca, the European war was first completely opened; notwithstanding all which had passed elsewhere, proposals for an accommodation of the American disputes were never discontinued, nor the war considered as universal, till that island was absolutely invaded. As for the captures at sea, the avowed cause upon which these were taken, sufficiently evince that they undoubtedly belong to the American war; they were made in consequence of the hostilities first commenced in America, and were seized as reprisals, for the injuries there committed upon the property of the people of England; as such they were always declared to be taken by the ministers of that kingdom, and the value of them to be on that account retained;* and upon application made to parliament soon after the seizure of them, the legislature expresly refused to distribute them among the captors, as they

* See the British declaration of war.

have

have done in refpect to all other prizes, which have been made fince the war of Europe began. But even if this diftinction, which puts the queftion out of all doubt, had not been made by the minifters of England, thefe captures furely can never be looked upon but as a part of the American war; it will not certainly be denied, that fuch a war may extend itfelf to the ocean, without having changed either its nature or denomination; what but captures at fea have been the great conftituent part of every American war before the prefent; as a war upon the American continent muft always be fupported by fuccours fent from Europe, it is abfurd to fuppofe that either party in this cafe would not endeavour, as far as he was able, to take or deftroy entirely the fhipping of his enemy, by which alone thofe fuccours could be conveyed. Countries which have very little internal force within themfelves, cannot be defended but by fuch troops as are thrown into them; to defeat, therefore, the only means by which this relief can be effected, muft be efteemed as material a part of fuch a war, as the means to inveft a fortrefs are a material part of a fiege. But after all, thefe captures were fubfequent to the reftoration of the port of Dunkirk, or the * preparations to invade Great Britain; and these can never be considered but as undoubted acts of aggression; it is not the first military action alone, but hostile preparations, where the design is apparent,† the usurpation of another's rights, or the denial of justice, which in the opinion of the ablest writers denominate the aggressor. The object of the defensive treaties are "rights, immunities, "and liberties," no less than "towns or "territories," and "the disturbance" or "molestation" of the former, as well as "the "attack" of the latter, are expresly declared to be cases within the guarantees.

A more subtle objection will still perhaps be made to what has been said. It will be urged, "that though France was the aggessor "in Europe, yet that it was only in conse- "quence of the hostilities commenced before

---

* Undoubted intelligence was received of this before the 27th August, 1755, when general orders were given to bring in French vessels; the Lys and the Alcide were taken on the coast of America, and are therefore in every light a part of that war.

† Quanquam et aliquando favor defensionis ad illius partibus stat, qui prior arma alteri infert, ut siquis hostem invasionis jam certum, per celeritatem oppresserit, dum ille adhuc in adparando bello est occupatus. Puffendorf de Jure Nat. &c. Lib. 8. cap. 6. sec. 3.

"in

" in America; with which it is determined
" by treaties, that Holland is to have no con-
" cern, and that the rights contefted at pre-
" fent are not contained in the guaranties."—
If the reafoning on which this objection is
founded was admitted, it would alone be fufficient to deftroy the effects of every guaranty,
and to extinguifh that confidence which nations mutually place in each other on the
faith of defenfive alliances: it points out to
the enemy a certain method of avoiding the
inconvenience of fuch an alliance: it fhews
him where he ought to begin his attack; let
only the firft effort be made upon fome place
not included in the guaranty, and after that
he may purfue his views againft the very object without any apprehenfions of the confequence; let France firft attack fome little
fpot belonging to Holland in America, and
her barrier would be no longer guaranteed:
To argue in this manner would be to trifle
with the moft folemn engagements. The proper object of guarantees is the prefervation of
fome particular country in the poffeffion of
fome particular power. The treaties above-
mentioned promife the defence of the dominions of each party in Europe, fimply and
abfolutely, whenever they are " attacked" or
" molefted." If in the prefent war the firft

attack was made out of Europe, it is manifeſt that long ago an attack hath alſo been made in Europe: and that is beyond a doubt the caſe of theſe guarantees.

Let us try, however, if we cannot diſcover what hath once been the opinion of Holland on a point of this nature.—It hath already been obſerved, that the defenſive alliance between England and Holland of 1678 is but a copy of the twelve firſt articles of the French treaty of 1662; ſoon after Holland had concluded this laſt alliance with France ſhe became engaged in a war with England; the attack then firſt began, as in the preſent caſe, out of Europe, on the coaſt of Guinea; and the cauſe of the war was alſo the ſame, a diſputed right to certain poſſeſſions out of the bounds of Europe, ſome in Africa, and others in the Eaſt Indies: Hoſtilities having continued for ſome time in thoſe parts, they afterwards commenced alſo in Europe; immediately upon this Holland declared, that the caſe of that guaranty did exiſt, and demanded the ſuccours which were ſtipulated. I need not produce the memorials of their miniſters to prove this; hiſtory ſufficiently informs us, that France acknowledged the claim, granted the ſuccours, and entered even into open war

in

in the defence of her ally : Here then we have the sentiments of Holland on the same article in a case minutely parallel : France also pleads in favour of the same opinion, though her concession in this respect checked at that time her youthful monarch in the first essay of his ambition, delayed for several months his entrance into the Spanish provinces, and brought on him the enmity of England.

If any doubt can yet remain about the meaning and intent of this article, it may farther be proved from the opinion of the Minister who made it :—Immediately after Holland was engaged in the war above-mentioned, she sent to the Court of France Monsieur Van Beuningen to press the execution of that guaranty, which he had himself concluded. It is remarkable, that in his conversations on this subject with Monsieur de Lionne, the same objection was debated against which I now contend : Van Beuningen treated it with great contempt; he asked Monsieur de Lionne,* if the pretence of the European war being only a continuation of that of Africa, was what the English alone alledged to deprive

* Lettre de M. Van Beuningen à M. De Witt, December 26, 1664.

them

them of the fuccours of France, or whether the French Minifter laid any ftrefs upon it as an argument at all to be fupported. De Lionne at firft gave him to underftand that he thought it of fome weight, " A quoi, je repondis," fays Van Beuningen, " que je ne croyis pas, " que cette objection fut ferieufe, puis qu' il " dit alors, que celui, qui a commence la " guerre en Guinneè, & de la en Europe, " n'a pas commencé de guerre en Europe; " & ne pouvoit paffer pour troubler la paix " & le commerce en Europe, parce qu' il " l'avoit troublé ailleurs auparavant:" and then he adds, " Ce, que j'ajoutai à ce raifon- " nement pour refuter cette objection, refta " fans replique." This was the fame Monfieur Van Beuningen who negotiated our defenfive treaty of 1678; he made the terms of both thefe guaranties precifely alike; and we before fhewed that our common cafe at prefent is exactly the fame as this on which his opinion hath been produced.

If, however, the words of thefe treaties had been againft the interpretation which hath been given them, I might juftly have appealed to the fpirit of them, as alone a fufficient foundation on which to build my opinion: The whole defign of all thefe our alliances
with

with Holland is to form a barrier against the power of those mighty kingdoms, whose ambition might otherwise induce them to destroy the independency of Europe: They are, in fact, a regular continuation of that policy which gave birth to the Triple Alliance, when the dangerous spirit of the French councils first began to appear. To answer this great end, they guaranty the possessions of those two maritime countries, who, from their wealth, their internal strength, and their incapacity of having any ambitious views themselves, are the best security against the designs of others: But as the obligations of these guaranties are too considerable to be made use of on trifling occasions, for this purpose the contracting parties have made one exception: The rights of the European kingdoms in the distant parts of the world, and particularly in America, are very uncertain, and the cause of frequent dissensions, and it is well known that wars have there subsisted for many years between the trading subjects and commercial companies of the several nations, while the mother countries have lived, if not in friendship, at least in peace; this then is the case particularly excepted from the guaranty; but this exception must always be so interpreted as to be made consistent with the principal intention of the alliance :---If some great country out of Europe should become of so much importance, that for the interest of Europe it ought to remain in the hands of the present possessors; if the same great disturber of mankind, after many fruitless attempts in his own neighbourhood, should now turn his thoughts another way, and should endeavour, by distant diversions, to enfeeble that power on whose consideration the safety of the public very much depends, and to deprive her of the sources of her wealth, which she hath always so largely expended in support of the common cause, would a generous friend, who attends to the spirit of his engagements, say, that the case of the guaranty did not then exist? and, when the reason of the exception is vanished, would he urge the pretence of it as an excuse for giving up the principal point on which the alliance was constructed?---But if to this distant attempt the enemy should add an open and avowed war in Europe, should threaten the mother country with invasion, attack her fortresses, and take occasion from thence to spread his armies over the continent, shall this pretended exception still be urged, when the literal case of guaranty is now become apparent? On this weak foundation shall a wise people, under such obligations,

tions, not only refufe to grant their affiftance, but not permit their forfaken ally to make a full ufe of his power? holding back in this manner his arm, when they will not ftretch forth their own, and claiming from the very contracts they have broken that privilege which they turn to the deftruction of her ally. The abfurdity is fhocking; fuch, however, is the prefent cafe of England: Unhappy in her friendfhips! She hath neither that affiftance from allies which they are bound by treaty to give her, neither is fhe allowed to exert even her own force, though abandoned to her own defence.

In this manner the point might be determined on a general view of thefe treaties; and this alone would be fufficient;—but it may be further proved that the article on which Holland founds her right of protecting the property of the enemy, as far as it relates to the prefent cafe, hath been particularly repealed long ago. The treaty in which this article was laft inferted was concluded the 1ft of December, 1674: Four years after this, in 1678, was paft that defenfive alliance, in which it was ftipulated between Holland and England, " that if either party fhould be at-
" tacked in Europe, the other fhould declare
" war

"war against the aggressor two months after he is required:" By this treaty, therefore, two months after England is attacked by France in Europe, Holland must become the enemy of the latter as well as England; and to be the enemy of another means certainly to distress his trade and seize his property, not to preserve the former and protect the latter. If this therefore is the right interpretation of the word enemy, this article directly and positively declares, that two months after France has attacked the European possessions of England, the ships of Holland shall not have a right to protect the effects of the French: this therefore is derogatory to the 8th article of the marine treaty of 1678, and as being posterior to it, absolutely repeals it. In all laws (and such are treaties in respect to nations) the last enacted always sets aside the former, so far as they disagree. Cicero * says, it ought to be considered, " Utra Lex " posterius sit lata, nam postrema quæque " gravissima."

But this maxim is not necessary on the present occasion, since the same article is again repealed by two subsequent treaties in words

---

* Cicero de Inventione.

as positive as can be used; for in that treaty,* by which all the old alliances between the maritime powers were renewed immediately after the revolution; and also in that of February 6, 1716, by which they were again renewed upon the accession of the present family to the throne, the treaties of 1674 and 1678 are expresfsly mentioned, and made of both a part; and it is there declared, that " they shall have the same force and ef-
" fect, as if they had been inserted in these
" treaties verbatim; that is to say, so far as
" they do not differ, or are contrary to one
" another; yet so as whatever hath been esta-
" blished by any later treaty shall be under-
" stood and performed in the sense therein
" expressed, without any regard had to any
" former treaty:" Can it then be doubted that the articles above mentioned are " con-
" trary to one another," as much as peace and war, as much as friendship and enmity? Is not the defensive alliance of 1678, " a
" later treaty" than the marine regulation of 1674? and ought not therefore, according to the words of the renewal, " the article of the
" latter to be performed in the sense therein

---

* Treaty of friendship and alliance between England and Holland, August, 1689.

" expreffed, without any regard being had to
" the former." Since then, the year 1689,
this article, as far as it relates to the prefent
cafe, hath been twice repealed.—Thus much,
therefore, may fuffice to fhew, that the right
of Holland in this refpect is extinct.

There remains one more claim to be confidered; a claim which, if report had not aver-
red that fuch a one had been formally offered, would by no means deferve an anfwer.
The northern crowns, whofe commercial
treaties with Great Britain contain not any
article which gives them exprefsly a right to
carry the property of the enemy, have endeavoured to deduce this right from a general ftipulation, which is to be found in fome of
their treaties, declaring, that " they fhall be
" treated in like manner as the moft favour-
" ed nation." If Great Britain therefore
hath granted by treaty to any other nation the
right, in time of war, of becoming the carrier
of her enemies, they think they are juftly entitled to be admitted to the fame favour. Under this pretence they claim this privilege, as
ftipulated in the Dutch treaty of 1674; but
it has been proved alfo that the treaty of 1674,
as far as it relates to the prefent cafe, is no
longer in force; if the inference therefore was
otherwife

otherwise just, the foundation being thus destroyed, whatever is built upon it must necessarily fall with it. But this stipulation of equal favour, from the very nature of it, can relate to nothing else but such advantages as may be granted to foreign traders by the municipal laws or ordinances of each country; such as equality of customs, exemption from the rigour of ancient laws, which would affect them as aliens, and the privileges of judges-conservators and consuls; these are the proper objects of favour, and because the whole detail of these could not easily be specified in a treaty, for this reason they are thus comprehended in a general article. If the rights conceded by treaties were the objects of this stipulation, to what purpose were any other articles added, since this would contain them all, and would alone include every privilege which past or future treaties could afford them? and can it be supposed, that any nation mentioned in this manner to preclude itself from the power of exchanging, by treaty, with some particular country, any great right of its own in return for an equal advantage? or that this right should, in such case, be universally forfeited to the people of every other nation, who would thus reap the benefit without having been parties to the bargain?

gain ? But this point is made clear beyond a doubt, from the words of the treaties themſelves, where this general equality is ſtipulated.

In the treaty of commerce between Great Britain and Sweden, of the 21ſt of October, 1661, (the principal one at preſent in force between the two countries) the fourth article, which contains this ſtipulation, plainly makes it refer to ſuch favours only, as may be enjoyed in matters of traffic within their reſpective dominions. The treatment which the contracting parties ſhall there give to the ſubjects of each other is the principal purport of the article; it ſpecifies many particulars, and among the reſt it ſtipulates, that the people of both countries ſhall have " liberty to im-
" port and export their goods at diſcretion,
" the due cuſtoms being always paid, and
" the laws and ordinances of both kingdoms
" univerſally obſerved;" and then, manifeſtly connecting this with what follows, it adds,
" which things being pre-ſuppoſed, they ſhall
" hold ſuch ample privileges, exemptions,
" liberties, and immunities, as any foreigner
" whatſoever doth or ſhall enjoy;" the general equality therefore here ſtipulated, plainly relates to thoſe places alone where the cuſtoms

toms of thefe kingdoms are to be duly paid, and the laws and ordinances of them are in force, and that is only within their refpective dominions. The privileges here conceded cannot poffibly have any larger extent; and to confine the fenfe of the article ftill more ftrongly to the explanation which hath now been given of it, the words, "in the domi- "nions and kingdoms of each other," are twice repeated, to determine clearly where that trade muft be carried on, to which this favour is meant only to be granted; if, however, any doubt could yet remain in refpect to this interpretation, they who made the treaty have given the ftrongeft proof, that under this article they never intended to imply a right of carrying the property of an enemy, fince, by the 12th article of this fame treaty, an attempt of that nature is pronounced to be "a heinous crime," and the ftrongeft provifions are made to prevent it. In the treaty of commerce between Great Britain and Ruffia, of the 2d of December, 1734, this ftipulation of equal favour is inferted in feveral articles; but it appears in every one of them, to relate to nothing elfe, but to the particular privileges which the fubjects of each were to enjoy while they were trading within the dominions of
the

the other. In the second article this equality is expressly said to be granted " throughout " the dominions of the contracting parties " in Europe." In the third it relates only to " the favourable reception of the subjects of " each other in the ports of their respective " countries." In the 14th it grants only an equal freedom to import " such merchandise " into each other's dominions as is allowed " to the subjects of any other country;" and in the 28th it refers only to the " respect and " treatment which is to be given to the sub- " jects of one party who come into the do- " minions of the other." In the treaty of commerce between Great Britain and Denmark, of the 11th of July, 1670, the latest at present in force between the two countries, the stipulation of equal favour is inserted in the 40th article; it is there said, " If the " Hollanders, or any other nation, hath, or " shall obtain from his Majesty of Great " Britain, any better articles, agreements, " exemptions, or privileges, than what are " contained in this treaty, the same and like " privileges shall be granted to the king of " Denmark and his subjects also, in most full " and effectual manner." That these privileges relate only to customs and other advantages of the same kind, might be proved

from

from the whole tenor of this treaty; but it will be sufficient to shew that the right of carrying the property of the enemy cannot possibly be intended by it. Holland had obtained this right in 1668, two years before the Danish treaty was concluded; if therefore the stipulation of equal favour contained in the 40th article could extend to an advantage of that nature, the merchants of Denmark would have been immediately entitled to it from the hour the treaty was signed: the ministers of that kingdom could not be ignorant of this; and yet in the 20th article they have positively forbid the exertion of any such right. They have even expressed the greatest apprehension, lest any liberty conceded by this treaty should be interpreted to that purpose; "lest such freedom of navigation," says the article, " or passage of the one ally, and " his subjects and people during the war, " which the other may have by sea or land " with any other country, may be to the " prejudice of the other ally, and that goods " and merchandises belonging to the enemy " may be fraudulently concealed under the " colour of being in amity; for preventing " fraud, and taking away all suspicion, it is " thought fit the ships, goods, and men, be-
" longing to the other ally, in their passage

"and voyage be furnished with letters of passport;" and in the passport the king of Denmark hath bound himself to declare that the ship and goods with which it is laden, " belong to his subjects, or to others having " an interest therein, who are the subjects of " neutral powers;" and that " they do not " appertain to either of the parties now en- " gaged in war." Nothing more, I hope, need be said, to refute this weakest pretence to a right of carrying freely the property of the enemies of Great Britain.

As there is no article, therefore, which grants a right of this nature at present in force in any of these commercial treaties, it is unnecessary to shew that most of the captures which England hath made of the vessels of neutral nations, ought not properly to be referred to it, but may be justified by another part of the said treaties, where it is declared,* " that all goods are contraband, which are " carried to places blockaded or invested."

The debate here would turn on the real existence of the blockade. To evince this, I

---

* Art. lxi. Treaty of 1674, between Great Britain and Holland. The same article is found in every other commercial treaty.

might

might shew what opinion the Dutch had of a naval blockade in 1630,* when they pretended to have blocked up all the coast of Flanders, and openly avowed that they would take and condemn all neutral ships which had the most distant appearance of being bound to the ports of that country. I might also shew their opinion of the same in 1689, when they declared † publicly to the neutral nations, that they designed to block up all the ports of France. I might observe, that as the possession of the principal avenues to a town constitutes a blockade by land; and that it is not necessary, for this purpose, to have made a complete line of circumvallation; so by keeping great squadrons of ships of war cruising constantly before the ports of an enemy, by destroying in this manner totally his trade, and preventing his fleets of war from ever venturing out, except now and then a ship or two by stealth, a blockade ought certainly to be considered as completely established by sea. I might farther prove the cause from its effects, and shew that the American islands at least have experienced all the consequences of such a situation; where want of communication with the mother country, distress, and

---

* Convention between England and Holland, 1689.
† Placart of June 26, 1630.

famine, fully declare that they have been invested. But as this topic may not perhaps relate to the cafe of every capture, and depends on the particular ftate of a variety of facts, I fhall not dwell any longer upon it at prefent. The queftion hath here, I hope, fufficiently been argued on principles which are plain and comprehenfive, on thofe equitable regulations which nature hath eftablifhed among nations, and on thofe particular contracts with which communities have bound themfelves. And as I before endeavoured to prove, that neutral nations had no right by the former of thefe obligations, to protect the property of the enemy; fo now it hath been fhewn by what policy the Dutch firft obtained this privilege; by what treaties it hath fince been taken from them; and by what conduct they have lately forfeited whatever might remain of this right. It hath alfo, I flatter myfelf, appeared with how little reafon other neutral powers, under colour of any article in their treaties of commerce, have claimed the enjoyment of fuch a right. Upon the whole, therefore, I will now beg permiffion to conclude, that the naval power of England hath been conducted, during the prefent war, with no lefs juftice than fpirit; that the faith of our fovereign is as fpotlefs as his courage; and that the honour of the country is unblemifhed.

The basis of just complaint being thus removed, those idle clamours which have been founded upon it, by no means merit our attention; to charge England with ambition, must appear so absurd to all who understand the nature of her government, that at the bar of reason it ought to be treated rather as calumny than accusation. Possessed of every blessing which civil government can produce, she is open to no temptation with which ambition might seduce her; pursuits of that kind might possibly operate to the destruction of her constitution, and her system of happiness might be subverted by the augmentation of her power. It must always be the interest of England to protect the just rights of commerce, and to support those principles which promote the labours of mankind, since she herself can only be great from the virtuous industry of her people. To obtain the largest extent from the exertion of this, is the point to which all her policy should tend; and if forsaking these maxims, she should seek to enlarge her power by any acts of ambitious injustice, may she then, for the welfare of the human race, cease to be any longer great and powerful! Her courts of maritime jurisdiction are more wisely calculated to preserve the freedom of navigation, than

than those of any other country; as they are not subject to the controul of her executive power, the paſſions of her princes or miniſters can never influence the deciſions of them; and foreign traders have in favour of their property all the ſecurity which the nature of the thing will admit, the conſciences of wiſe men determining upon matters of right, whom the threats of power cannot affect, and who are ſet free, as far as poſſible, from all bias and partiality; and to the honour of the learned perſons who at preſent perſide in thoſe courts, one impartial teſtimony ſhall here be produced in their favour. Though treaties have expreſsly pointed out to all who may there think themſelves injured, a regular method of redreſs before a ſuperior tribunal, the merchants and freighters of Holland have never ventured as yet to bring to a hearing, or even to put into a way of trial any one of the appeals which they have made from the determinations of theſe judges, giving thereby cauſe to preſume that they made them with no other intention but to delay the execution of the ſentences; and conſcious of the invalidity of their rights, they have in this manner plainly confeſſed the real equity of thoſe deciſions which have been paſſed upon them. That amid the confuſions of war, ſome irregulari-

ties

ties may be committed, is a misfortune too true to be denied, but which the circumstances of the case render impossible to be wholly prevented. They are the consequences of all wars, not alone of the present. To destroy the trade of the enemy, it is necessary to employ privateers, which cannot always be kept under those strict rules to which a more regular force is subject; these maritime hussars may sometimes exceed their commissions, and be guilty of disorders, the authors of which cannot always be punished, because the nature of the fact renders the discovery of them difficult. But can the crimes of these be imputed to ministers, whose ears are always open to complaints, and who labour, as much as possible, to redress them? The privateers of England are already made subject to every restraint, which naval policy hath as yet invented to force them to conform to their duty. If, however, these are found insufficient, and if any more successful means can be discovered to prevent every unjust depredation, by which the evils of war may be diminished, confident I am, that Great Britain will be the first to adopt them; let them be consistent only with the use of her naval power, and conformable to justice, the British legislature will enact such into a law, and

the

the British ministry will attend most steadily to the execution of them.

But after all, the wisest regulations on occasions like this cannot be expected to answer fully the end proposed; the system of humanity is no where perfect, but in respect to nations its weakness is most apparent; the softer ties of natural affection among these have little effect, and no coercive bands of power exist to regulate and controul their passions; it is the virtue of government alone, on which the general prosperity depends, and treaties have no better sanction than what that virtue can give them. These were the principles from which I first commenced my discourse; by these the rulers of communities are instructed to amend, as far as possible, by their prudence, what nature hath left imperfect. Ambition or avarice will augment the evil; moderation may prevent it. Every little inconvenience must be patiently suffered where a superior right makes it necessary. The love of our country should never induce us to act contrary to that love which we ought to bear to mankind, since the interests of both, if they are rightly pursued, will always be found consistent with each other.

FINIS.

New Publications Printed for J. DEBRETT.

THE PARLIAMENTARY REGISTER; or, The HISTORY of the PROCEEDINGS and DEBATES of both HOUSES of PARLIAMENT: Containing an account of the moſt intereſting Speeches and Motions, authentic Copies of all important Letters and Papers laid before the Houſe during the preſent Seſſion.

⁂ NUMBERS I. and II. of the PRESENT SESSION, publiſhed this day, contain, among many others, the much-admired SPEECHES of the EARL of MORNINGTON, Mr. PITT, Mr. FOX, Mr. SHERIDAN, Mr. SECRETARY DUNDAS, &c. &c. on the ADDRESS to his MAJESTY.

‡‡‡ This Work was originally undertaken at the Deſire of ſeveral Perſons of diſtinguiſhed Abilities and Rank, from whoſe communications and patronage it has derived peculiar advantages. The favourable reception it has met with during the THREE LAST and preſent Parliaments, while it demands the moſt grateful acknowledgements of the Editors, encourages them to proſecute a continuation of the ſame during the preſent Seſſion. For this purpoſe, they beg leave again to ſolicit the aſſiſtance of all their former Friends, and every other Gentleman. A ſtrict attention will be paid to all their commands and favours; nor will any aſſiduity or care be wanting to preſerve that truth and accuracy for which this Work has hitherto been diſtinguiſhed.

Of whom may be had,

The PARLIAMENTARY REGISTER of the FIRST, SECOND, and THIRD SESSIONS of the preſent Parliament, in Nine large Volumes Octavo, Price 4l. 4s. half-bound and lettered.

The PARLIAMENTARY REGISTER, from the General Election in 1780, to the Diſſolution of Parliament in 1784, in Fourteen Volumes, Price 5l. 5s. half-bound and lettered.

The PARLIAMENTARY REGISTER, from the General Election in 1784, to the Diſſolution of Parliament in 1790, in Thirteen Volumes, Price 6l. 12s. half-bound and lettered.

The DEBATES and PROCEEDINGS of both HOUSES of PARLIAMENT, from the Year 1743, to the Year 1774, in Seven large Volumes Octavo, Price 2l. 9s. in Boards.

The

New Publications Printed for J. DEBRETT.

The CASE of LIBEL, the King v. John Lambert and others, Printer and Proprietors of the Morning Chronicle, with the Arguments of Council and Decision of the Court on the general question, " Whether the Special Jury in a " Cause, first struck and reduced according to the statute, " shall be the Jury to try the issue joined between the " Parties?" Price 1s. 6d.

The CASE of the WAR CONSIDERED, in a Letter to Wm. Duncombe, Esq. Member of Parliament for the County of York. By a Yorkshire Freeholder. Price 1s.

Mr. FOX's LETTER to the Worthy and Independent ELECTORS of WESTMINSTER, the Thirteenth Edition. Price 1s.

A LETTER to the NOBILITY, CLERGY, and GENTRY of FRANCE, now resident in England, on the Present Crisis. Price 1s.

The MERITS of Mr. PITT and Mr. HASTINGS, as MINISTERS in WAR and in PEACE, impartially considered. " The experience of all ages and countries " teaches us that calumny and misrepresentation are fre- " quently the most unequivocal testimonies of the zeal, and " possibly the effect, with which he, against whom they " are directed, has served the Public." Mr. FOX's Letter. Price 2s.

An AUTHENTIC REPORT of the IMPORTANT DEBATE in the HOUSE of COMMONS, May 6 & 7, 1793, on Mr. GREY's MOTION for a REFORM in PARLIAMENT, containing the Speeches on that interesting Question at length; to which is annexed a correct Copy of the PETITION of the FRIENDS of the PEOPLE. Price 2s. 6d.

A TOPOGRAPHICAL DESCRIPTION of the WESTERN TERRITORY of NORTH AMERICA; containing a succinct Account of its Soil, Climate, Natural History, Population, Agriculture, Manners, and Customs; with an ample Description of the several Divisions into which that Country is partitioned.

By GEORGE IMLAY,

A Captain in the American Army during the War, and a Commissioner for laying out Lands in the Back Settlements.

To which are added, The DISCOVERY, SETTLEMENT, and PRESENT STATE of KENTUCKY; and an ESSAY towards the Topography and Natural History of that important Country. By JOHN FILSON.

Also,

New Publications Printed for J. DEBRETT.

Alſo, 1. The ADVENTURES of Col. DANIEL BOON, one of the firſt Settlers; comprehending every important Occurrence in the Political Hiſtory of that Province.

2. The MINUTES of the PLANKASHAW COUNCIL, held at Poſt St. Vincent's, April 15, 1784.

3. An ACCOUNT of the INDIAN NATIONS inhabiting within the Limits of the Thirteen United States; their Manners and Cuſtoms; and Reflections on their Origin. The Second Edition, with conſiderable Additions, illuſtrated with correct Maps of the Weſtern Territory of North America, and the State of Kentucky, as divided into Countries, from the lateſt Surveys, with a Plan of the Rapids of the Ohio. Price 6s. in Boards.

⁎ The above Work contains intereſting Information reſpecting the moſt œconomical and expeditious Method of travelling into the interior Parts of America, directing the Meaſures to be purſued in purchaſing Land, and guarding againſt the Impoſitions which have long been practiſed by Land Jobbers, to the Ruin of many honeſt Settlers. And, as impoſitions have proved more ſucceſsful, from a belief generally entertained by Purchaſers, of the extraordinary Fertility of all the Soil upon the Waters of the Ohio, it particularly deſcribes that Diſtrict of Country, and points out the Veins of good and bad Land in every Part of the Weſtern Territory of America.

REPORT of ALEXANDER HAMILTON, Eſq. Secretary to the Treaſury of the United States of America, on the Subject of Manufactures. Price 2s. 6d.

The AMERICAN BOOK of COMMON PRAYER, and Adminiſtration of the Sacraments, and other Rites and Ceremonies, as reviſed and propoſed to the Uſe of the Proteſtant Epiſcopal Church, at a Convention of the ſaid Church, in the States of New York, New Jerſey, Pennſylvania, Delaware, Maryland, Virginia, and South Carolina, held in Philadelphia, from September 27 to October 7, 1785. To which is added a Collection of Pſalms. Price 4s. in boards.

PLAN of the NEW CONSTITUTION of the UNITED STATES of AMERICA, agreed upon in a Convention of the States, with a Preface by the Editor. A new Edition. Price 1s.

COMMENTARIES on the CONSTITUTION of the UNITED STATES of AMERICA, in which are unfolded the Principles of Free Government, and the

ſupe-

New Publications Printed for J. DEBRETT.

superior Advantages of Republicanism demonstrated. By James Wilson, LL.D. Professor of Law in the College and University of the Commonwealth of Pennsylvania, one of the Associate Judges of the Supreme Court of the United States, and appointed by the Legislature of Pennsylvania to form a Digest of the Laws of that State; and by Thomas M'Kean, LL.D. Chief Justice of the Commonwealth of Pennsylvania. The whole extracted from Debates published in Philadelphia, by T. Lloyd. Price 3s.

TRANSACTIONS of the AMERICAN PHILOSOPHICAL SOCIETY, held at Philadelphia for promoting Useful Knowledge, 2 vols. 4to. illustrated with several Engravings. Price 1l. 16s. in Boards.

⁎ The Third Volume of this Work is in the Press, and will speedily be published, and may be had as above.

HISTORY of the FRENCH REVOLUTION. To which is added, Political Reflections on the State of France; and a Chronology of the principal Decrees and remarkable Events during the Sitting of the Constituent National Assembly. Translated from the French of J. P. RABAUT ST. ETIENNE. By JAMES WHITE, Esq. The Second Edition. Price 5s. in Boards.

" We have no Doubt of the Fidelity of Mr. White's Translation; and we cannot but think, that even those Persons who are unfavourably disposed towards the French Revolution, may be entertained and informed by the Perusal of this Volume.

Monthly Review, App. to Vol. viii. 1792.

" We have transcribed much from this Author, who deserves greatly our Regard and Attention. It is an able Narrative, generally specious, and often judicious."

Critical Review, October, 1792.

LETTERS from PARIS, written during the Summer of 1791 and 1792, illustrated with an elegant Engraving, representing the Capture of LOUIS XVI. at Varennes, in 2 Vols. Price 12s. in Boards.

" We have perused these Letters with a great Degree of Pleasure, and can recommend them with Confidence to our Readers, who will not be disappointed in them; whether they look for a fair and accurate Account of the principal Transactions that have taken Place in France during the last two Years, or who would wish to become acquainted with the State of Arts, of Literature, or Learned Men, in a Country where they have lately been exposed to so much Danger and Neglect.

European Magazine, June, 1793.

www.ingramcontent.com/pod-product-compliance
Lightning Source LLC
Chambersburg PA
CBHW020153170426
43199CB00010B/1019